PRAISE FOR O

Out of the Shadows, a compilation of stories of American military women who served in combat, is an eye-opening account of what it is *really* like to be a woman in a man's world.

The narratives reveal the true courage, strength, tenacity, and leadership exhibited by nine heroic women who share how they fought internal as well as external battles through Iraq and Afghanistan, through doubt, fear and loss, through disabling injuries, amputations and post-traumatic stress.

We learn not only about the innumerable obstacles each faced in the brutal battle to transition back to civilian life but also about their ongoing challenges of living in a civilian world post combat.

These are real women, representative of thousands of sister warriors, who have earned the respect of not only their military peers but of countless grateful Americans.

— EILEEN HURST, FOUNDER AND
FORMER DIRECTOR OF THE VETERANS
HISTORY PROJECT, CENTRAL
CONNECTICUT STATE UNIVERSITY

I love this book! In Ron Farina's masterful hand, these women's harrowing, poignant tales of courage and perseverance will inspire you and touch your heart. Farina's storytelling—the elegant prose combined with the breakneck pace—creates a page-turner as compelling as any great novel. After reading these female veteran's stories, I feel as if I know them. I wish I could meet them to personally thank them for their service.

—JANE K CLELAND, AGATHA-AWARD WINNING AND BESTSELLING AUTHOR OF CONTEMPORARY FICTION AND NON-FICTION

In his first book, *Who Will Have My Back*, author Ron Farina captured the voices of caregivers to disabled veterans. He has done it once again in *Out of the Shadows: Voices of American Women Soldiers*. This time the author provides an up close and personal look at women soldiers who served our nation in Iraq and Afghanistan. In *Shadows* the author has amplified, acknowledged, and honored the voices of these women, capturing their bravery, sacrifice, and resilience. These stories are inspirational and moving.

— NOEL SO, MD, AMPUTEE REHABILITATION SPECIALIST, DENVER, COLORADO

These stories are so immediately compelling, it only takes one step and you are inside that world, not as a reader, not as an observer, but there, as one of the soldiers and battle buddies as they face incredible challenges. You can feel the heat, taste the dust, and smell the fear. This is as real as it gets—virtual reality via the written word. Ron Farina's talent at storytelling is incredible. He pulls you into this world and gives you an insider look at what women soldiers do, think, feel. Their voices are in your head and their stories stay with you.

— MAJ. GEN. MARI EDER, U.S. ARMY
(RET.), FORMER COMMANDING
GENERAL OF U.S. ARMY RESERVE JOINT
AND SPECIAL TROOPS SUPPORT
COMMAND

Ron Farina's book engagingly captures the narrative of modern American soldiers who served and sacrificed in battle. At times uplifting, and at times heartbreaking, these are real stories of women warriors that must not be ignored. Their experiences and struggles should be a reminder that our country has an obligation to fulfill its promise to honor and support our post-9/11 generation of veterans.

— LT. COL. AMY MCGRATH, USMC (RET.)

OUT OF
THE SHADOWS

—— Voices of American Women Soldiers ——

Ron Farina

with the support of Duke Leopold d'Arenberg

Published by Lagrange Books, an imprint of Oren Litwin
Visit our website at https://lagrangebooks.com
Contact us at editor@lagrangebooks.com.
Sponsored by the Arenberg Foundation.
Visit our website at https://www.arenbergfoundation.eu

This is a work of creative nonfiction. Some dialogue has been reimagined for narrative purposes. Some events have been dramatized, but are presented substantially as they were described to the author.

Cover design by Deranged Doctor Design:
https://www.derangeddoctordesign.com

Map of Southwest Asia by United States Central Intelligence Agency: https://www.loc.gov/item/2001623732/.

Map of Iraq by United States Central Intelligence Agency, Cartography Center: https://www.loc.gov/item/2003629862/.

Map of Afghanistan by United States Central Intelligence Agency, Afghanistan Administrative Divisions: https://www.loc.gov/item/2009575509/.

Photos of, or concerning, the subjects of the book were provided by them. We thank them warmly for their permission to use the images, and their courage.

OUT OF THE SHADOWS

VOICES OF AMERICAN WOMEN SOLDIERS

RON FARINA

This book is made possible by the generosity of HSH Duke Leopold D'Arenberg.

Crest of the House of Arenberg

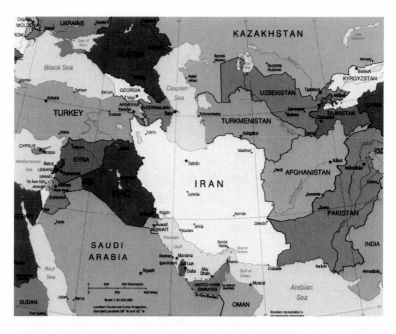

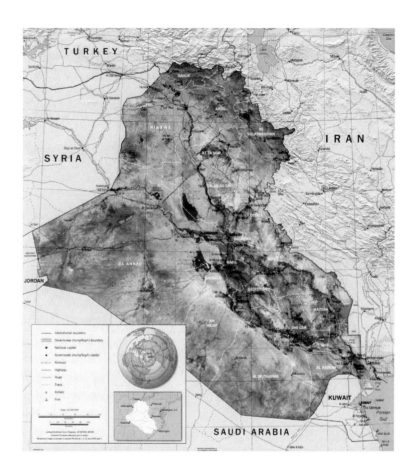

CONTENTS

FOREWORD

DR. LINDA SPOONSTER SCHWARTZ, USAF (RET.)

Prior to 1980, very little was ever said or written about America's military women, and even less was known about them. Although women have served honorably in every major American war since the founding of our nation, their roles were mostly behind the scenes, ordinary, or "Freeing a Man to Fight." Until 1970, Federal law actually limited the number of women permitted to serve to no more than 2% of the active-duty force. Even before the ban on women in combat was lifted in 2013, hundreds of military women had already served in Iraq and Afghanistan. Many had been wounded and killed in action. But maintaining the façade that military women were never in harm's way was more important than giving them the credit. In 2015, Defense Secretary Ashton Carter opened all military occupations to women. The "rules of engagement" had changed significantly. If you think you know war, think again!

Out of the Shadows is a new narrative of the experiences, service and sacrifices of nine American women soldiers in the 21st century. The voices of our "Lady Vets" recount their personal experiences transforming from civilian to soldier, practicalities of living and surviving in combat areas and dealing with the aftermath of war and their military service. Author Ron Farina takes us on a journey into the hard-core, no-frills realities of everyday life for women in combat zones and convoys of Iraq, Kuwait, Afghanistan, and surrounding environs—Forward Operating Bases, life-and-death tempo of Combat Support Hospitals and Army Trauma Centers.

One has to appreciate the bond of trust Kendra, Connie, Marlene, Vivian, Mary Jessie, Jennifer, Maggie, Tara, and Lana had in Ron Farina to faithfully recount their journey. Ron's attention to details, imageries and exquisite melding of the voices of our Lady Vets with the individuals that populate their stories create a truly unique experience. Readers of *Out of the Shadows* are truly privy to the "stories soldiers rarely tell." We thank you for your service, we thank you for your sacrifice and most of all, we thank you for your TRUTH!

> **When I stand before thee at the day's end**
> **Thou shalt see my scars and know**
> **That I had my wounds**
> **And also my healing.**

—Rabindranath Tagore, in *Stray Birds*

—Dr. Schwartz was President Obama's Veterans Affairs Assistant Secretary for Policy and Planning, the first woman to hold that position. The disabled Vietnam veteran served 16 years in the Air Force and 11 years as Connecticut's Commissioner of Veterans Affairs, also the first woman to hold that position.

INTRODUCTION

HSH LEOPOLD, DUKE OF ARENBERG

In January 2021, I agreed to support the publication of *Out of the Shadows: Voices of American Women Soldiers*. By then, the U.S. had been at war in Afghanistan for close to two decades, having first entered Afghanistan to defeat al-Qaeda in October 2001, following the terrorist attacks of September 11th. A little over two years later, on March 20, 2003, the U.S. invaded Iraq. That war lasted almost a decade, running concurrently with the war in Afghanistan until the U.S. declared its end to combat hostilities in Iraq on December 15, 2011. Thousands of U.S. service members died in the wars in Afghanistan and Iraq; tens of thousands were wounded.

Many of the dead and wounded are women.

When I finally put my hands on this book, I found myself deeply touched by the experiences of the American women soldiers chronicled in this collection. Many women were asked to tell their stories. What appears on the pages of this book are the stories of nine wounded women soldiers who agreed. Too many of the stories of American women soldiers have gone unwritten. I hope you, the reader, will discover as did I that the stories, as powerfully described in this book, reflect the heroism and sacrifice of America's Women Soldiers.

At least 152 women soldiers have died in the wars on terrorism. Over a thousand more have been wounded. During the duration of the Iraq War and for the greater part of the war in Afghanistan, American women soldiers were officially kept out of direct combat roles, serving in the shadows of their male counterparts. Unofficially, however, women served bravely in combat, for almost two decades—a reality that everyday Americans were unaware of.

Banned from roles in the infantry, women served as Military Police, Civil Affairs Specialists, and in Intelligence, Transportation, and Explosive Ordinance. In war, all these roles, no matter how circuitous the route, connect directly to combat. Those connections are clearly defined in each of the stories in this collection.

Not until December 2015—when Secretary of Defense Ashton Carter announced that all military occupations and positions, combat roles included, were open to women—did women soldiers officially gain the same recognition as their male counterparts. Still, their sacrifice often goes unnoticed.

Even though the day each one of them was wounded was a long time ago, those stories still have the power to bring back dark memories for each of these women. Soldiers will tell you: some stories are better left untold. But it is only through the telling and re-telling of these stories that readers like you and I can begin to understand the heroism and sacrifice of the American woman soldier.

I do not take for granted the telling and re-telling of their experiences; no one should. It takes a different kind of courage to revisit the battlefield, long after the dust has settled, and the din of battle has gone silent. The women in this book had the courage to revisit the battlefields of Afghanistan and Iraq, all so that readers everywhere may gain a better understanding of what it means to be a woman soldier.

I want to thank very much the author of this book, Ron Farina, for his dedication, involvement and great efforts. This project was a daunting challenge and he brought it to fruition. For me personally, playing a part in bringing these stories to readers everywhere has been an honor and a privilege.

This won't be the last time someone asks these women to tell their stories. And when they're asked again, most of these women soldiers will take a deep breath, gather themselves, and softly, slowly, they'll answer our questions, yours and mine. Listen carefully.

—Duke Leopold d'Arenberg

To the American Woman Soldier, this book is for you. You've always known what the rest of the world should understand. Women acquit themselves on the battlefield, doing so with courage under fire.

—R.F.

Connie

SADDLE UP

It's boots and chaps
It's cowboy hats
It's spurs and latigo
It's the ropes and the reins
And the joy and the pain
And they call the thing rodeo.

— GARTH BROOKS, "RODEO"

SEVENTEEN-YEAR-OLD CONNIE NEILL waits in the alley—"the hole" or "the shoot," some call it. She's saddled up on Lady, her twelve-year-old chestnut mare, a thoroughbred/quarter horse mix. Lady is a big horse for barrel racing. What she might give away in agility, she makes up for with speed. Connie wears Wrangler jeans cinched with a turquoise-beaded belt and silver rodeo buckle. A Western shirt, mother-of-pearl snaps, embroidery decorating the shoulders and chest, is tucked into her slim waist. A black Stetson, pulled low, hides her eyes. A long black braid sways like a pendulum across her back and shoulders. Cowboy boots with pointy toes, roach killers, complete her rodeo outfit.

Rider and horse are a team. They've worked together for years. They know each other, have confidence in each other, trust each other. Lady knows what's expected, she'll do what Connie asks. She'll run for Connie, not out of obligation, but because she wants to. She starts to sweat, tosses her head back, looks over her shoulder, all anticipation. Her muscles tense. A shudder runs through her body. Connie strokes Lady's neck, leans low enough to whisper in her ear. Lady settles, ready now to thunder out of the alley.

Ground conditions are good, sandy, without slick spots to worry about. Flags gently flutter on a light breeze. The announcer is loud, but there's no blaring music. "You're gonna like this, Lady, it's a good ring. You ready?"

Lady paws at the dirt.

Connie closes her eyes. She takes in the smell of the arena, Lady's sweat, the sounds of the announcer, the crowd, leather complaining as she twists her hips, getting positioned in the saddle. A constant reminder from her dad runs through her mind, "Keep your heels down, girl, heels down."

The announcer's voice raises above the roar of the crowd, "Next up, Connie Neill."

Connie opens her eyes. It's time.

On cue, Lady bolts forward, her hooves send dirt flying. Connie is low, leaning forward. Horse and rider gather speed. Connie tosses her Stetson to a nearby cowboy just before Lady explodes into the rodeo ring at a full run, chasing the cans. Connie shifts her right knee forward, up near Lady's shoulder, her left foot instinctively slides back behind Lady's girth, toward her haunch. Lady understands, responds. Horse and rider angle well for the first barrel, turn quickly and line up for the second. They shoot for the third and make the run back toward the entrance. Connie deftly snatches her Stetson from the cowboy holding it up high. She reins Lady to a halt. It's a good run, one of their best. One of their last.

Several months later, Connie landed at Camp Doha, in Kuwait, quickly moving into Camp Udairi, the jump-off point into Iraq. By early spring of 2003, the mild Kuwaiti winter turned hot. The sun blistered the ground. Temperatures soared. Staging for the rollout into Iraq became a mind-numbing, repetitive routine, worse in 100-degree-plus heat. Days blurred: up at 0530, chow, formation, work on Humvees, weapons maintenance, drill, get ready to roll out.

Caught in the hurry-up-and-wait, the archetypal motif of all things military, trained for action, constantly on edge, soldiers grew restless. Rumor was they'd be rolling into Iraq any day, but the hurry-up-and-wait was mostly wait, punctuated with harassing Scud missile attacks that sent Connie and her fellow soldiers scrambling. When the missiles, rumored to contain gas, rained down, shouts of "Gas! Gas! Gas!" replaced shouts of "Incoming," a more common refrain of previous wars, particularly the Vietnam War. Well over one hundred soldiers scrambled into metal shipping containers, packed in together, "asshole to belly button." Connie was one of the first —a mistake. The doors slammed shut. Everything went black. In the dark, listening to explosions all around her, mask on, protective gear on, pushed to the rear of the container, squeezed, jostled and bumped by dozens of other soldiers, almost all men, Connie prayed she wouldn't have to inject herself with atropine, either in her leg or heart. In the dark, heart racing, sweating, her breathing labored and loud inside the mask, Connie waited. The attack went on for more than thirty minutes. Eighteen-year-old PVT2 Connie Neill, sobbed into her mask. She felt a fear so deep that it changed her life forever.

"This is it," she thought, "this is it. I'm going to die."

When she'd enlisted, spurred on by the patriotic clamor for revenge after 9/11, restless for life beyond high school and the farm, not interested in college, Connie was like most women and men joining the military: young, invincible, and naïve. The reality of combat was an abstract, until . . .

But the gas, another one of Saddam's propaganda boasts, was an empty threat. The danger of exploding Scuds, *that* was real and potentially lethal. Metal shipping cans offered little or next to nothing in the way of protection from the exploding missiles.

Off duty, she wrote letters, watched movies, played video games. More than once the order, "Ready your gear, vehicle, and person, we're moving out in the morning," was rescinded with the command to "stand down." And then on April 1st—

Connie heard the command, "Saddle up, we're moving out."

April 1st. The Fools' Day. Perfect.

Soldiers, fueled on adrenaline, ran to Humvees that roared to life, belching diesel exhaust. The convoy formed. Shouts of "Let's go kick some Iraqi ass," could be heard over the roaring Humvees. Radios crackled; soldiers cheered. The order, "Move out," loud and clear sent the convoy rolling. The Humvees gathered speed, roared down the alley through the opening in the fifteen-foot-high berm, concrete barriers, and wire surrounding the camp. They blasted into Iraq like Lady exploding into the ring—at a full run. Inside her Humvee, in the saddle, Connie held the reins as they crossed into Iraq. Her team, last in the almost one-hundred-truck convoy, provided security. Rear guard.

Through the noise, the smells, the dust, Connie understood—she'd been preparing for this moment since she was a little girl learning to rodeo. Rodeo and working with Lady had taught her so much: respect, patience, responsibility for something other than herself. She'd cared for Lady. Together they ran barrels, chased cans, asked and gave of each other. Lady became her partner. The partnership was their bond, the rodeo their family.

This, this, these soldiers, they're my partners, the Army, it's my family now.

The convoy rolled into Iraq. Everywhere she looked, Connie saw signs of the war. Cars on fire. Bombed buildings reduced to piles of rubble. Damaged, destroyed or disabled Iraqi tanks dotted the horizon, and what could have been bodies. She wasn't sure.

"So, this is what war looks like," she thought. "This is the cost of war."

Nervous chatter inside the Humvee surrendered to the silent monotony of hours of dust-filled driving. In the silence, lost in her own thoughts, Connie wondered about family back home. She missed them.

Raised by her dad, the youngest of five children, she'd grown up in South Dakota. Her mom left before Connie turned seven. Maybe five kids, a farmer husband, maybe that life was too hard for her. Maybe there was something else. Her dad never talked much about it. Connie knew enough not to ask. The kids stayed with him. Connie was ambivalent about her mom's indifference.

When she came to her dad and told him she wanted to join the Army, John Neill, an aging veteran of the Korean War—a man who often struggled with what to say to the girl who'd suddenly become a woman—paused from his work, blew out a deep breath, and told his daughter what he thought she needed to hear.

"It ain't something you can quit," he said.

Near dusk, the convoy reached a predetermined rendezvous, a rally point on the journey into Iraq. They bivouacked for the night, forming a perimeter with the trucks, like pioneers circling wagons. Some of the Humvees, ragtops, even had canvas covers. Tracer rounds from firefights off in the distance zipped back and forth, a lethal crisscross dance that shredded the night sky. Flashes from the heavy artillery blazed brilliantly on the horizon. The fireworks of war, lethal, brilliant, mesmerizing.

One hundred trucks—fuel and water tankers, supply trucks, Humvees. Hundreds of men. Two women. Privacy for men wasn't much of a concern during convoy missions. Convoys won't risk too many roadside stops, so when nature calls, men were quick to hop out of the Humvees, take care of business, mount up, and roll out.

When the convoy did stop, Connie and her battle buddy, Sarah, a diminutive gunner on a second Humvee, gave each other cover behind Connie's Humvee, the last vehicle in the convoy. Thankful for the small bit of privacy, Sarah and Connie shed their battle gear, dropped trousers, squatted and peed into the sand. It wasn't always that easy. Sometimes, Connie was the only woman. She often chose to drink less, even in the extreme heat; that way she could delay the call of nature. She refused to use a GoGirl, an obscene contraption that allowed women to relieve themselves while standing without removing their trousers. Either practice led to urinary tract infections and more. The only other option was to have one of the men stand with his back to her.

Inside the perimeter they'd set up with their vehicles, Connie, Sarah, and the men ripped open MREs, the modern-day version of military C-rations. Connie kept the wet wipes. Toilet paper, she quickly learned, could be hard to find.

Connie and Sarah slept next to each other on G.I. folding cots that sank into the sand. They slept in their uniforms, their SAWs under the cots, 9mm strapped to their legs. Connie loosened her belt, untied her boots to give her feet a little comfort.

Friends now; but just weeks earlier, Sarah and Connie had barely spoken to one another. From different parts of the country, Sarah from urban Florida, Connie from rural South Dakota, the two teenage women had little in common. Connie, the tall, soft-spoken country girl with brown eyes and long dark hair, was open and approachable. Sarah was the polar opposite, short, blue eyes, light hair, a facial expression that appeared angry or contemptuous, maybe both. The tension between them, palpable, was short lived. Connie was pulled into the platoon office and ordered to get along with the new private.

Weeks later, the two women, after receiving the necessary security clearances for their work as Military Police, went to breakfast together, becoming friends over pancakes. The friendship blossomed when they found themselves the only two women in a platoon of twenty-four. Sarah joined Team A. Connie drew Team B. Connie didn't know it yet, she couldn't, but Sarah would be there for her. Sooner, it turned out, than anyone might have imagined.

On the morning of the second day in Iraq, after break-fasting on MREs, Sergeant Marshall, Private Cooley and PVT2 Connie Neill—Team B—mounted up. Sergeant Marshall, a gentle giant of a black man, Team B leader, took the reins of the Humvee. Cooley was a black man too. Connie, from South Dakota, had barely met anyone of color, and had no idea what to expect. The two men treated her like a little sister. Sergeant Marshall, Connie discovered, had the same birth date as her father, John Neill.

Their target, an FOB on the grounds of the Musayyib Power Plant on the banks of the Euphrates River, was almost a full day's ride. The convoy formed up; one hundred trucks belching diesel exhaust and fumes rolled forward on a narrow two-lane dirt road, gathering speed. Sarah and

Team A moved in behind the convoy, close to the rear, Sarah in the gunner's turret. Sergeant Marshall rolled up, taking the last position in the convoy, "Tail-End Charlie." The throaty roar of the huge convoy built to a blaring crescendo.

At random intervals, the Humvees would break from the chain of vehicles, surging ahead to the left and alongside of the convoy, checking, looking for disabled vehicles, bad guys, and general mayhem. Closer to noon Sergeant Marshall drifted out from the rear, reaching the middle of the convoy. In the distance, he spotted a rising dust cloud. The radio crackled. A returning medical convoy carrying American wounded was heading south toward yesterday's rally point. Marshal slowed and took up the Tail-End Charlie position once again, prepared, once the medical convoy reached them, to make certain they could pass.

Dust from the opposing convoys billowed into the air. The dirt road grew soft and powdery. *Sand. Deep sand.* Tires churned up more dust. Visibility diminished like a South Dakota winter whiteout. The convoy, bogged down in the sand, stopped without warning. The Humvee, short and thick-set, ran into the rear of a much taller, immoveable water tanker. The front of the Humvee vanished beneath the larger truck, crashing abruptly. The Humvee's windshield and roof slammed into the truck's thick steel bumper.

The force of the impact threw Connie forward. She heard a crunching, crackling sound. Bones in her nose fractured. She had slammed her face into an empty GPS bracket that pushed its way underneath the rim of her Kevlar, splitting her forehead open, exposing bone. Blood spurted from her nose. The gash on her forehead bled into her eyes.

She blacked out. Cooley and Marshal too.

In and out of consciousness, Connie caught a glimpse of Sergeant Marshall slumped over the steering wheel. Cooley was behind her. She felt hands lift her, pull her from the damaged Humvee. She vomited all over herself and the soldier. Someone asked if she was okay. Sarah?

Connie lost consciousness again. Personnel from the medical convoy, doctors or medics, Connie would never know for certain, rendered first aid. They collared her neck in a soft brace, slid her onto a spinal board, securely strapping her on, asking her what day it was, what her name was, if she knew where she was, keeping her awake, loading her into an MEV.

Hours later, back at yesterday's rally point, doctors got a better look at her.

"Hey soldier," a lieutenant colonel with a caduceus insignia said, "This is your lucky day. Back in the real world, I'm a plastic surgeon. I'm going to take care of that forehead of yours. No one will notice it after I'm done."

Still fading in and out of consciousness, Connie was loaded onto a Blackhawk helicopter, stacked with other wounded soldiers on a system that looked like a bakers pan rack, and medevac'd back to Camp Arifjan in Kuwait. Stacked above all the other soldiers, nauseous again, braced and strapped, Connie managed to tilt her head slightly, just enough to vomit into her hair, on her chin and cheek, and the soldier below her. Her broken nose began to bleed again. She thought *this is not what I signed up for* then passed out again.

At the CSH (combat support hospital), doctors, unable to diagnose the extent of Connie's head injury, waited a day then decided to transfer her to Landstuhl, Germany where the Army had MRI equipment. Connie, conscious now and fearful that she'd never get back to her unit, hesitated.

While doctors deliberated, a woman Connie never saw again, whose name she never knew, washed her hair, cleaned the vomit from her neck, the blood from her face. Later Connie talked a medic into removing the brace from her neck. The nagging headache she'd dealt with since regaining consciousness began to diminish. Beginning to recover, she left the CSH the next morning. Fortunate to have her ruck and gear with her, she found an open barracks, showered, changed into clean clothes and slept. Hours later, she woke, lay on her side, and watched naked men walk down the center aisle of the barracks.

Ten days later, stitches removed, face healing, looking more like the squared-away soldier that she was, Connie met an officer from the 101st, her unit. He arranged for her to fly with him to the FOB at Iskandariyah, where she found her team, Sarah, Sergeant Marshall and Cooley. When they spotted her, their chins dropped, mouths gaped open, riveted in disbelief.

"Hey," Connie shouted, "what's a girl gotta do to get one of you guys to carry her gear?"

Marshall, Cooley, and Sarah wrapped their arms around Connie.

Marshall crushed Connie in a bearhug, lifted her off the ground and spun in circle. "I didn't think we were going to see you again," he said.

The FOB at Iskandariyah, not much more than another rally point, boasted little in the way of comfort. No showers. Latrines, discarded, rusty, sawed off fifty-five-gallon barrels with a toilet seat nailed to a board that straddled the barrel, provided minimal privacy and even less comfort. A poncho teepee, open at the top, surrounded the barrel. More than once, Connie looked up to see a Blackhawk gunner waving to her, giving her a thumbs up, visor raised, a grin on his goggled face.

Life quickly became a mindless routine. Most of Army life is. The Military Police Teams patrolled the perimeter, guarded POWs, and stood watch at the opening in the wire, waiting in one-hundred-plus degrees on top of their Humvees. Connie, skittish about driving the Humvee since the accident, moved to turret gunner. Whenever Team B pulled a mission outside the wire or stood guard at the gate, she mounted a belt-fed M249 light machine gun into the turret, slid a pin through a connecting hook, then snapped the disintegrating link belt into the machine gun.

Hours later, when they'd roll back through the wire, a mission complete, Connie would unhook the SAW, hop from the Humvee, and saunter away, the machine gun resting over her shoulder at a jaunty angle. Men would watch and whisper. Just nineteen, in the best shape of her life, a country girl from farmland South Dakota with a swagger, she looked provocatively badass.

She was.

In middle school, when she'd begun rodeo, Connie trained Lady and herself for months before John Neill, a man who knew horses and riders, felt that his daughter was ready— ready, but untested. For every cowgirl, cowboys too, there's a first time. When the announcer shouts her name, when it's time to explode into the ring that first time, that's when a cowgirl finds out what she's made of. It's a question only she can answer. Connie had been trained well by the Army. The Army, just like John Neill, knew that she was ready—ready, but untested.

All that was about to change.

Team B, queued up in rotation, pulled gate security on a routine basis. No one expected anything different when they rolled up to the gate, relieved Team A and took up position. Connie, in full battle rattle, perched in the turret, looked out over the horizon. Cooley shut the Humvee down, pushed open the driver's door, slid back in the seat and rested a foot on the door hinge. Sergeant Marshall leaned against the open passenger door.

Shimmering heat waves blurred the horizon like a fun-house mirror. An hour passed. The three soldiers exhausted small talk, and then—movement in the distance—small group —looks like bad guys—maybe armed.

Marshall swung his M4 to the ready. Cooley pulled the Humvee door closed. Connie swiveled the machine gun, pushed the safety and cocked the slide hammer. Pinpricks of heat needled her neck. Her heart raced.

"Get those bad guys in your sights, Neill," Marshall ordered.

Connie instinctually levelled the sight on the Iraqis. When she had the lead bad guy in her crosshairs, she slid her fingertip from the lip of the trigger guard. She felt for the curve of the trigger. With a touch as light as a feather, she kept the finger against the trigger while keeping a bead on the lead Iraqi, ready to fire on command. The Iraqis, local friendlies, raised their hands above their heads. Connie kept them in her crosshairs.

Marshall investigated. Connie continued to watch, ready to shoot if necessary. After a lot of arm waving, pointing, hand gesturing, Marshall turned the Iraqis away. Connie watched them shuffle off. In that moment, she answered the question for herself and everyone around her. She could do whatever was needed. She was ready to protect her men . . . a badass country girl who could *man up!*

A few weeks later, Marshall completed his tour of duty while Team B was still in Iskandariyah. Before he left, he pulled Connie aside. "Let me give you a few more tips on how to stay safe," he said, "cause I ain't gonna be here to take care of you, and bring you home safe. It's on you, Neill, it's on you now to keep yourself safe," he said. "One more thing, Neill."

"What?" Connie said.

"I'm proud to serve with you."

When Marshall returned stateside, he left the Army. A

short time later, he contacted John Neill. "Sir," he said, "your daughter is a good soldier."

Women, men, supplies, and equipment moved through Iskandariyah. The FOB, a small base, functioned as a staging area, temporary POW detainee center, a rally point and jump-off to parts of Iraq north of Baghdad and deeper in country. Connie's unit, the 101st Military Police Company, moved to Mosul by early summer.

Initially holed up in a smaller FOB, a compound surrounded by wire, Connie and the rest of her unit trained men to become part of an Iraqi police force. A short time later, they moved onto the larger airbase at Mosul. The airbase, with showers, indoor plumbing, segregated barracks, hot chow, gave everyone a chance to clean up. Able to wash their hair, put on clean uniforms and walk around the base in combat fatigues and t-shirts, take better care of themselves, women could be more feminine.

Mail that could not reach soldiers on remote FOBs and small compounds reconnected them with home. Not all of it was good. Dear John letters were common. Barriers fell. Lonely men and women looked for companionship. Tensions between men and women, tensions that had been absent out in the field, became more commonplace on the comfortable airbase.

The Company split into smaller units. The mission changed. From here on out the 101st rolled with supply convoys from Turkey to Mosul, providing security. Connie, a rear turret gunner, protected the convoy's six. Under constant threat from Iraqi insurgents, always in harm's way, Connie up until now had managed to avoid any firefights, and even the more common, often-lethal IED attacks.

By late fall into early winter, temperatures moderated to a

more tolerable eighty degrees. Scheduled to rotate back to the States in late January or early February, Connie breathed the rarified air of the short-timer. She'd be home soon.

Convoys traveling on routes that had become predictable became easy targets. Two main bridges over the Tigris River, about two klicks from the gate, emptying traffic onto the airbase at Mosul, didn't provide much of a choice. When the security teams, usually consisting of three or four up armored Humvees, rolled out on their way to pick up a convoy, they'd usually egress the area after routes closer to the base had been swept for IEDs. The teams returning, especially after dark, faced a greater risk.

During the first week of January, on a Tuesday, just three weeks before the 101st was scheduled to rotate home, two teams from the 101st, accompanied by two Humvees from the 10th Mountain Infantry, headed back to the airbase after safely escorting a general to his destination. Already late in the day, the night sky enveloped them as they neared the Tigris River, about three klicks from the safety of the base. Rolling up on the Tigris, they chose the same route, the same bridge that they had crossed earlier in the day. Foolish. Predictable. Dangerous.

Connie, rear gunner on the last Humvee, scanned rooftops, the side of the road, buildings, abandoned cars, looking for anyone and anything behind them that might pose a threat. Insurgents disguised IEDs and hid them everywhere —in trash piles, cars, even animal carcasses.

The 10th Mountain Humvees, one and two, rolled onto the bridge. In the dark, the front gunner had little chance of spotting an IED—or the insurgent watching and waiting for the security detail to cross the bridge. Vehicle three rolled onto the bridge; the insurgent held his breath, waited a split second longer, then pressed the trigger on a remote detonator just as vehicle four, Connie's Humvee, rolled onto the bridge.

Connie had looked left, right, shifted her gaze to a rooftop, then back to the disappearing road behind her. She looked right again. The night exploded with a brilliant flash. The explosion lifted the third Humvee, in front of Connie. Its turret gunner took the full brunt of the blast. Shrapnel clawed through his face, tearing and ripping flesh and bone. He began to choke on blood filling his mouth—his own blood.

Connie, facing away with her head turned to the side, felt a sudden sensation on her neck like a thousand bee stings. Slammed forward, almost knocked unconscious, she slumped down into the turret tower, not fully certain of what had just happened. Then, just as quickly, she understood she'd been hit. She tugged at her chin strap and pulled off her Kevlar, her helmet. She slapped at the side of her face. Her Keffiyeh, the large scarf she wore around her neck, was wet. Odd. She pulled it across her face and over her head, ripping it off. Shrapnel had run its hot jagged edge from the back of her neck to a hair's breath away from the carotid artery, opening a deep gash that bled freely. Blood from the Keffiyeh covered her face, streaked her hair. She touched the side of her face. Her flesh burned, a feeling like she was on fire.

"Oh my God, not my face, please, not my face."

The Humvees stopped. Uninjured soldiers poured from the vehicles, going tactical, setting up kill zones, ready for a ground assault that might follow the IED attack. Sergeant Ferrel, a red-haired woman warrior who'd replaced Marshall, pulled Connie from the Humvee. She tore open a field bandage, pressed it against the gaping wound on Connie's neck, keeping it closed—not knowing if the shrapnel had nicked the carotid artery, hoping for the best.

Connie's body reacted to the loss of blood, the impact of the blast, the trauma of the attack. Blood vessels, signaled by the brain to conserve blood flow, narrowed. Blood pressure dropped. Connie slipped into shock. The pain dulled. Her mind played tricks. In the confusion, she pictured herself in the imaginary town of Greenbow, Alabama, Forrest Gump's hometown.

She heard Jenney yelling to Forrest. *"Run Forrest, run," Jenney shouted. They disappeared through crops of tobacco, into a corn- field. Jenney dropped to her knees, pulled Forrest down with her. "Pray with me Forrest, pray with me."*

Over and over, Connie heard the words, *"Dear God, make me a bird, so I can fly far, far away from here."* Over and over, a continuous loop, fast forward, rewind, the scene and the words played back. The escort detail reformed, covered the three klicks back to the airfield, rolling up to the CSH with Connie and the other wounded.

Medics slid Connie onto a stretcher, carried her into the CSH, and laid her down on a surgical table. Still bleeding; her face was now a mask of blood.

"Pray with me Forrest, pray with me. 'Dear God, make me a bird, so I can fly far, far away from here.'" A surgeon bent low. Connie heard his voice. "Hold on, soldier."

Tears tracked through the blood on her face.

"Those are some pretty big crocodile tears," the surgeon said. "I've got you. You'll be okay. You'll feel better in a minute. We're going to give you something."

Morphine flooded through her body. The movie stopped. Forrest and Jenny faded from view. They began cutting off her uniform, removed her dog tags.

I must be dying, she thought. *Why else would they take my dog tags? They're gonna toe tag me. I don't want to die. I want to see my family. This will be too hard for them . . .*

Everyone in the surgical unit shouted orders. Organized chaos. Someone slipped a mask over her mouth. Everything began to move in slow motion. Voices muted.

She woke the next day to find a Purple Heart pinned to her pillow. She panicked. *I need to call home,* she thought. *What if someone has reached out to Dad? He'll think the worst. He'll worry. I've got to call him.*

An E-5 sergeant named Massey, the ward NCO, had a satellite phone. Connie called her dad. No answer. The only other number she could remember belonged to her brother John. He picked up on the third ring. When she heard his voice, when he said his name, she tried to speak, managed a few sorrowful words, and began sobbing.

She was rescued by Sergeant Massey. He calmly explained to Connie's brother that she had been injured, wounded. "She's alright, safe, in good hands, and will recover," he said. Connie tried again, but couldn't speak to her brother without crying.

In less than a week, she left the CSH, and returned to her unit. Soldiers, her battle buddies, said nothing about her injury or the IED attack. Connie, not even old enough to buy a beer in most states, understood that this was how it was supposed to be. Putting her emotions on display would only continue to make her look weak—at least that's what she believed.

Her Purple Heart went unrecognized by unit commanders. Instead of talking about the attack, she said nothing, bottled up her feelings and slid back into her turret, wanting to be like Rambo, tough, impregnable, a warrior's warrior. Stoic. Emotionless.

The trauma of the attack wasn't about overcoming fear, or the loss of invincibility, a feeling that often tags along after a soldier is wounded. Those things she accepted. She was a soldier. She was back in harm's way just ten days after the roadside bomb almost killed her.

What haunted her, the up-close reality of war, was the idea that someone had tried to kill her: that lethal intimacy, its sudden consequence for those she loved. *That's* what overwhelmed her, that's what she feared. Suddenly lonely, wanting more than anything to be with people she loved, understanding that if something happened to her, it would devastate her dad, her brothers and sisters—that made her vulnerable, and afraid. With no one to talk to (nobody goes to psych without jeopardizing their security clearance or a return to duty), she stuffed her emotions in a box.

Four weeks after the attack, after rejoining her unit, after resuming missions, the wound on her neck still angry, Connie Neill rotated stateside.

A return from war—even with today's modern Army programs of mandatory transition time before leave, before going home—asks a lot of a soldier. You can remove her from the battlefield, bring her home, that's one thing; but removing the battlefield from the soldier, that's something altogether different.

The self-preservation skills—every discarded piece of trash is a potential bomb, every image lurking in the shadows is an insurgent with an RPG, every hillside or bend in a road or path is a perfect place for an ambush—asking a soldier to turn off her Spidey sense, that's a big ask.

On leave before reporting back to Fort Campbell, driving her new truck, Connie continued to scan rooftops and buildings. Debris on roadways accelerated her heartbeat, made the hairs on the back of her neck stand up. Loud, sudden noises brought her back to the moment the roadside bomb exploded. She never watched the movie *Forrest Gump* again.

Her remaining time at Fort Campbell was uneventful, almost. Garrison duty for military police is the equivalent of being a civilian police officer. Respond to disturbances, investigate complaints, monitor traffic, catch speeders. One particular traffic stop remains to this day something Connie recalls with anger and amusement. A colonel recently returned from Iraq, blasting around the base in a little white compact car (probably a rental), took particular umbrage when Connie pulled him over.

He began berating her. "How dare you pull me over, *Specialist* Neill," he said, looking at her name tag. "What the hell do you think you're doing?" He spat out the word "Specialist" as if to emphasize the disparity in their rank, trying his best to intimidate her.

"You were speeding, sir," Connie calmly replied.

"So what? I just returned from Iraq, and you're going to pull me over for speeding, for speeding? I'm a colonel in the United States Army, maybe you didn't notice?"

Connie, only recently returned from Iraq herself, the wound on her neck still raw, flushed with anger. *What a jackass, using his time in Iraq to alibi his bad behavior. Control yourself, girl, control yourself.*

"Give me just a moment, sir. I'll be right back," she said. "I'll take care of this for you."

In her police vehicle, she took about thirty seconds to make a decision. She walked back to the car, the colonel smiling, thinking he'd dressed her down, certain that she was going to apologize. She politely handed him a speeding ticket.

"Have a nice day, sir," she said, saluted, and walked back to her squad car.

By the spring of 2005, Connie's enlistment was nearing an end. She was ready to leave. The life of a woman in the Army, not really ideal for marriage or starting a family, always moving around—that wasn't the life she had in mind. She was a good soldier. The Army wanted her, but no amount of convincing from the base Reenlistment Officer would change her mind.

Early that summer, her enlistment completed, she went home.

Trained for combat or policing, Connie didn't have a lot

of career options. By 2007, she had married, given birth to a little girl, and divorced.

For the second time in her life, she thought, *This is not what I signed up for.*

Nerve and tissue damage to her face, numbness in her neck, became constant reminders of the attack. Whenever she drove her truck, or rode in someone else's car, she worried. Her eyes and ears, her sense of smell, told her that she was safe, home. Her mind said something else. Whenever she heard a loud noise, she flashed back to the night that the IED explosion ripped open her neck. A trash can on the side of the road, ready for pickup, instantly brought her back to Iraq. No matter what would trigger the panic and fear, what flashed through her mind was always the same. She relived the explosion, the flash, the sound. Worst of all, she could feel the impact to her neck.

When she'd been attacked and wounded, more afraid to appear weak, she denied herself permission to understand what had happened to her. The rational Connie Neill knew that she was home, knew that she was safe. But she struggled to understand what had happened to her in Iraq, and why, almost every day, she was reliving what had happened to her. She hadn't asked for help, hadn't said the bad parts out loud, something no one had encouraged, but she needed to make sense of her past and what was happening to her now.

Life was about to change for the better. A friend urged her to get some help. She did. The right people came into her life at the right time. Three veterans from Wounded Warrior Project, Craig Meissen, Jonathan Robertson, and Joe Fox, befriended her. They'd all served. She trusted them. They had her back from the moment they met her.

She could talk with them. They understood. They'd been there, done that. With them, it was a judgement-free zone. When she said, "Being a soldier is easier than being a veteran," they got it. She still jumped at loud sounds, still scanned the horizon, still felt the impact of the wound to her neck whenever she looked into a mirror—but she wasn't alone anymore. With Craig, Jonathan, and Joe, she could say the bad parts out loud. They helped welcome her back from the war, changed her life, and in August of 2007, the former high school rodeo star, the girl who'd never been much of a student, enrolled at South Dakota State University.

While attending university, out one night with a few friends in a local bar, she eyed a tall, good-looking guy. *Do I know him?* She and he frequented the bar, began recognizing and nodding to each other. Even though she didn't remember him, they'd gone to the same high school, hailed from the same town, Elkton, South Dakota. They'd both served. Shawn, a former Marine, had left Elkton after high school, two years ahead of Connie. He returned a short time after she left for the Army.

They liked each other and began dating. When Shawn Johnson asked her to become his wife, Connie said yes.

Connie earned a B.A. in Education and Human Services, majoring in Human Development and Family Studies. She interned with a local social services group, then went to work for them as a Family Services Specialist. She first worked in the Child Protection Department. A short time later, she took a position in the Department of Corrections, working as a parole agent.

She wanted more.

She navigated her way through graduate school, earned a master's degree in Counseling and Human Resource Development. Her paper, "The Invisible Student"—a short thesis dealing with veterans on campus, their often-difficult transition, and the isolation veterans often feel in the midst of younger students—caught the eye of the Veterans Affairs

Resource Center on campus. Connie was encouraged to apply for a vacant position. When she was offered the role of Coordinator for Veterans Affairs at South Dakota State University, she accepted the position.

Working with veterans would become her vocation and her redemption. The days are busy, full, and sometimes challenging. Connie wouldn't have it any other way. This is where she belongs. She's doing what she was meant to do. She's doing what she loves. She's helping returning soldiers.

She's made SDSU a formal Purple Heart campus. She founded the university's Team Red, White & Blue program, a veteran-support nonprofit organization whose mission is to increase the connectivity between America's combat veterans and people in their communities. No returning veteran should feel isolated. She's become a Warrior Leader for Wounded Warrior Project. She is the Purple Heart commander for the Department of the Dakotas, North and South Dakota Purple Heart chapters. Her message when she meets a troubled veteran is simple, direct and heartfelt: "It's okay. It's okay to feel dark and lonely, it's okay, but believe me—believe me when I say tomorrow, it will get better. You're in the right place."

***

Thirty-seven-year-old Connie Johnson parked her pickup in the driveway after a day at the university. Out of the truck, she crossed the short distance to the pasture gate, then rested a booted foot on the bottom rail of the fencing. In the distance, a chestnut mare raised her head. Her ears pricked forward. She paused, recognized the familiar sound and casually walked toward Connie. Connie reached up and rubbed the horse's forehead. She slid the palm of her hand, down the horse's broad neck. The mare bobbed her head up and down, then pushed her muzzle forward, exhaling a deep fluttering breath through her nostrils. Connie slipped her a treat.

"I'm happy to see you too," Connie whispered, "You ready for a ride girl? It's a beautiful day, nobody'll be home for hours. I'll change."

When she returned, Connie wore blue jeans, cowboy boots, a worn and tattered 101st Screaming Eagle baseball cap, and a black t-shirt. A long black braid draped itself over her right shoulder. She saddled the horse, slipped a foot into a stirrup and swung herself up, settling lightly onto the saddle. The horse turned her head. Connie bent low, whispered, "Let's go."

They headed east. About a mile out, Connie guided the horse through a small creek and into a large grassy field. She stopped, remembered. "You were born when I was in Iraq. Did I tell you that before? I probably did. I had your picture near my cot, hung it up with a few others. My dad helped Lady bring you into the world. He named you Angel.

"I miss my dad, Angel. I miss him."

Connie felt the coolness of the approaching night through her t-shirt. She turned Angel to the west, heading into the sunset and home.

Kendra and Sky

FINDING HER VOICE

Find your voice and use it . . . take chances . . . never give up.

— *KRISTIN HANNAH,* THE FOUR WINDS

FROM KENDRA'S vantage point just offstage, the ballroom room looked full, more than packed. People stood in the aisles. Just a few days earlier, she'd been asked to speak at this fundraiser, a gala event. Reporters, cameras hanging from their necks, crowded the no-man's-land between the stage and the first row of seats. On stage, off to the left, the important people sat on folding chairs, preening for photographers.

Kendra began to have second thoughts. Maybe this hadn't been such a good idea.

Meredith Iler, chairman of Texas-based nonprofit Helping a Hero, walked to center stage, took up a position behind the podium, and tilted the microphone to a comfortable level. Her touch set off an echo that reverberated through the room, followed by screeching feedback. Her nose wrinkled. She quickly stepped back. A sound technician hurried to the microphone, made some mysterious adjustment, nodded her approval, and turned the stage back to Meredith.

She recovered quickly, made a joke, and began recognizing state and local politicians, veterans in the audience, their families, local business leaders—all potential donors. Done with the obligatory formalities, hoping she hadn't neglected to mention anyone, she looked to her right, then back to the audience in front of her.

"Ladies and gentlemen," she said. "It's my honor to introduce one of America's heroes, Army Sergeant Kendra Lou Garza."

The lights in the ballroom dimmed. Everyone on stage stood. Meredith moved to the side of the podium, waiting. Offstage, Kendra didn't move. She clutched a few pieces of paper. Notes, not very many, were scribbled across the pages. She wore a HelpingaHero.Org polo shirt. The stitched sleeves of the shirt, tight against her muscled upper arms, reflected hours spent in a weight room. Loose-fitting black slacks hid the prosthetic she wore in place of a missing left leg. She'd been working hard at getting back in shape, thankful that she'd pushed past the pain during rehab, when muscles had screamed at her to quit.

Her face flushed. A trickle of sweat raced down the center of her back, making her shiver. Her mouth felt as dry as the Trans-Pecos Chihuahuan Desert. Unconsciously, she held her breath. *You better breathe, girl,* she told herself. *If you don't, you're gonna pass out.*

Meredith beckoned. Kendra crossed the stage and reached the podium, her limp noticeable to the few people who knew her story. The two women embraced. Kendra settled in behind the podium. She reached for the microphone, which, still under the technician's spell, behaved itself.

"I'm Kendra," she said, her voice cracking. "How y'all doing?" The audience responded with polite applause, settled, and waited.

"I'm super nervous," Kendra said. "I even had to remind myself to breathe. They tell me you all want to hear about me.

I don't know why anyone would want to listen to me talking and telling my story? I'm just Kendra from a small town in Georgia. I'm way out of my territory here in Texas. But here goes."

For the next thirty minutes—longer if you counted all the questions everyone wanted answered—Kendra found her voice.

There's a lot of places to begin a story. Kendra is a pretty woman, thirty-four-years-old, she's a daughter. She's been a wife. She's a mother. She's been a soldier. She's been wounded in combat. That last—the day she almost died in Afghanistan —*that* changed her life forever.

She began her story there . . .

In late spring of 2010, the weather in Afghanistan had already reached one hundred degrees. Even for someone like Kendra, accustomed to the hot summers of small-town Monticello, Georgia, that's hot.

On Combat Outpost Charkh, Kendra, off duty, relaxed in front of one of the lady soldiers' tents. She cleaned an M4 long gun, the standard weapon for American military police and brigade combat teams. She carried a pistol too, not unusual for an MP. A shadow darkened the ground in front of her. She looked up and recognized the NCO in charge of her squad.

"Hey Sergeant, what's up?" she said.

"I'm taking the squad outside the wire. There's a bunch of Taliban in the village. Word is they are planting IEDs, maybe planning an ambush. The mission is voluntary."

"Who all's going?" Kendra asked.

"The whole squad. We're going to provide security for EOD engineers. We're off duty today, but the brigade is stretched thin. They can use the extra support."

"I'm in," Kendra said. "If my squad's going, I'm going too. Where we headed?"

"The village just outside the wire. We'll be on foot. Saddle up. We head out at 1200."

"Roger that, Sergeant."

The squad sat near the HQ tent, saddled up in full battle rattle, waiting. Clouds rolled in. The day turned gray, the air heavy. Kendra could hear the call and response of a firefight on the other side of the village, the crisp rhythmic pops of AK-47s, answered by the bass burping of the M4s. "It's close," she thought.

The engineering detail was late.

Waiting gave her time to think. Waiting is the enemy of a soldier's calm. Waiting unsettled her. She grew apprehensive. Call it a soldier's intuition: this mission wasn't going to be just another walk in the park. She could feel it, gray day, lots of activity outside the wire, extra squads saddling up. Trouble.

They knew the area well, patrolled outside the wire almost every day. There were plenty of places for Taliban to hide, to watch, to wait, to detonate an IED, then ambush with small-arms fire. The engineers' success depended upon the squad's ability to protect them.

Kendra was just a few days away from her twenty-second birthday.

By 1300 hours, the squad, with the engineers in tow, left COP Charkh. Outside the wire, the senior NCO, more familiar with the surrounding area, walked point, leading the patrol away from frequently traveled and more predictable routes into the village. Kendra was second man up. They climbed up and over a mud wall, stepped through a small stream, waded through a deeper river. The route, deliberately circuitous, an attempt to confuse Taliban insurgents, took them through a sparsely wooded area on the outskirts of the village.

They entered the village on high alert. The sergeant

signaled to stagger the formation. The patrol moved cautiously, scanning doorways, windows and rooftops. Expecting to find women selling flatbread, men bartering for goat meat, chai vendors brewing tea, they entered the village bazaar, the hub of commerce and activity. *Empty.*

An elderly man fingering a *tasbih*, a string of Muslim prayer beads, quickly ducked into an open doorway, disappearing behind an ill-fitting, weather-beaten, wooden door. The patrol turned onto a familiar track, a footpath they called "Route New York." Missing were the smells of baking flatbread, roasted meats, nuts, tea—all of it replaced by the smell of fear. Silence fell over the deserted bazaar like a heavy, wet blanket.

They walked by alleys. Left. Right. Figures darted across one of the alleys. Kendra counted three. One stopped, locked eyes with her. She began to raise her rifle. He fled. Kendra, raised two fingers, pointed at her eyes, then to the alley, then to the men behind her. She held up three fingers. They nodded, signaling that they understood. She wanted to scream, to shout at everyone, "Take cover!" But shouting would just tip off the Taliban.

No longer a question of "Is something going to happen?" Kendra understood it was only a matter of what, where, and when: an RPG attack, a small-arms assault, a remotely detonated IED.

Something's going down, she thought. *Something's going down.*

The patrol pushed forward, turning down a dirt footpath. A Hajji in his white pilgrim's robe, praying in front of a mud hut, spotted the patrol and ran away. The foot path narrowed. The sergeant leapt across the opening of an alleyway on the left. He motioned to Kendra to hug the wall, creep up on the alleyway, whirl, point and clear. She breathed deeply. A shadow flitted across the mouth of the alley. Spooked her. She looked down at fresh tracks in the dust. Sights, sounds, smells, everything around her intensified. Her chest involuntarily tightened. Her heart raced. Fighting against a sudden shortness of breath, she inhaled from the pit of her stomach.

Stepping forward with the well-practiced caution of a combat soldier, she looked for trip wires. Lift the foot slowly, place the heel down first—gingerly—walk on eggshells. None of that mattered to the Taliban waiting in the shadows, watching. Using a cell phone, he triggered the IED hidden in the wall that Kendra had pressed herself against for cover.

The blast, a rush of air traveling at the speed of sound, paralyzed her for a split second, then hurled her into the air, lifting her high above the ground. Deafened by the explosion; everything happened like a silent movie. Her eyes involuntarily closed against the flash of the bomb. Time suspended. She could feel herself falling in slow motion.

She slammed into the ground. The impact forced her eyes open. A plume of debris mushroomed above her. Dust, gravel, metal fragments, splintered bone, blood—her blood—rained down on her face.

Take a War Pause, Kendra. Do it, she told herself. *Take the five seconds. Assess.*

She heard small-arms fire, looked for her M-4. *Gone.* She thought about reaching for her Beretta 9mm. *The rest of the squad must be injured. I can't—I can't see anyone through this dust.* Her eyes, filled with dust, blood vessels ruptured by the blast, felt like they were on fire. *Check yourself. Pat down. I don't feel my leg. Holy shit it's me. I'm the one wounded—I'm wounded. Blood on my hands, flesh too. My leg. It's gone. Gotta stop the bleeding. Tourniquet. Left cargo pocket. Get it. My leg's gone. My pants too. No tourniquet. Gotta stop the bleeding somehow. Sit up. Use both hands. Apply direct pressure. Do it, Kendra. Do it!*

She clamped her hands around what was left of the rest of her leg, the few remaining inches just below her hip. She squeezed with all the strength she had left, slowing but not stopping the bleeding. Without help, she would bleed to death, and soon. She felt tired. Closed her eyes, letting sleep tiptoe in. A slap jolted her awake.

"Don't you die on me, soldier!" Medic Flynn, the newest woman member of the team, shouted. "Stay with me, Goddammit. It's my first mission in country. Stay awake, you hear me, stay awake!"

A second medic from a nearby scout patrol arrived. Together, the medics secured a tourniquet around what was left of Kendra's leg, stopping the bleeding. They started a battlefield IV. Kendra looked up.

They've got me. I'm okay now. I can rest. She relaxed, closed her eyes, drifted off. Another slap. She opened her eyes. *Why the hell are they slapping me? I don't want to see any of this anymore. I don't like all this noise. Are we in a firefight? This is the last place I want to be. Afghanistan is crazy. I'm just going to rest a while, get away from all this noise and craziness. I'll just sleep. Sleep . . .*

In and out of consciousness, the scene around her played out like intermittent static on an old television. She'd pass out, the screen would go black, wake up to a fuzzy image, catch a glimpse of the show, then pass out again. Members of the squad lifted her onto a litter, rushing her out of the firefight. They ran with her to a hot LZ, set the stretcher down, formed a perimeter around her, returning fire, waiting for the dust-off. A medevac, a Black Hawk helicopter about to land, suddenly veered off. Tracer rounds from the firefight had set the clearing on fire. Someone covered Kendra with a fire blanket.

Soldiers lifted her again. They ran to the river. Kendra bounced on the litter. The Black Hawk hovered above the river bank, machine guns blazing. They'd need to hoist Kendra to safety—quickly. A litter dangling on the end of cables, descended slowly. A soldier reached up, grabbed the litter, finally within reach. Kendra, strapped on, looked up at the bottom of the Black Hawk. The litter began a slow ascent, rising slowly through the air—a perfect target. Helpless, all Kendra could do was wait, and hope.

Without warning the litter began to spin uncontrollably, twirling like a pinwheel in a hurricane. The cable twisted and knotted to the breaking point, stopped spinning for a second, then uncorked in the opposite direction, spinning wildly once more. The force knocked Kendra unconscious. The medevac crew fought the spinning litter, wrestled Kendra into the Black Hawk, brushed off from the battlefield. They flew to FOB Shank, the closest CSH: Kendra's original home base, and her best chance for her survival.

On board the Black Hawk, she opened her eyes. Two medics feverishly worked on Kendra, their faces hidden by Darth Vader-like masks, masks that kept their microphones from being washed out by rotor and wind noise. One of the medics pushed a syringe of Ketamine into the IV. In a minute, Kendra closed her eyes.

The Black Hawk set down. Medics and doctors rushed to the helicopter. The entire camp ringed the landing area. They cheered when Kendra, conscious again, raised an arm, stuck a thumb into the air, then disappeared into the CSH. Twenty-four hours later, she woke in a hospital bed at Landstuhl Regional Medical Center (LRMC), the largest American military hospital outside the continental United States. They would save her life.

For three days, she would wake, pass out, wake again, and try to piece together the fragmented blur of conscious moments, before passing out. When she woke again later, much later, she opened her eyes. A nurse tending to her IV noticed.

"You're awake?" the nurse said. "Don't cry, you're safe."

"Will I still be able to have kids?" Kendra said.

"I don't see why not."

Kendra passed out again.

Doctors, too busy trying to save her life, had no time to clean the blood, shrapnel, gravel, and dirt from her hair. They ordered a nurse to shave her head. The wife of one of the officers stationed at the hospital intervened. Tall, blonde hair so light, it almost looked white, always with red lipstick. Everyone knew her as Miss Amy.

"Hey soldier," she said. "If it's okay with you, I'm going to clean you up. You're going to be heading back to the States. Your mom will be waiting. You don't want her to see you like this, do you?"

Kendra nodded.

Gently, patiently, Miss Amy washed Kendra's hands, gingerly cleaning each finger, cleaning blood and dirt from beneath every fingernail. She turned her attention to the rest of Kendra. She washed her—washed her hair, washed it again. Slowly, deliberately she combed pieces of metal out, blood and dirt, then dried and brushed her hair. Tears covered Kendra's face.

The crowd in the ballroom grew quiet, stunned into silence by what they'd just learned. Kendra felt the beginning of tears, faint thin lines barely noticeable. In all the time since she'd been injured, she'd never said the quiet part out loud. She'd never said to anyone, "I only have one leg." Saying it meant that she'd have to accept it. She hadn't. She'd never grieved for the loss of her leg. There, on stage, the reality hit home. She'd opened a Pandora's box. Tears, just storm clouds moments earlier, now rained down her face.

The crowd, on their feet now, erupted with applause. Led by Meredith, Kendra stepped in front of the podium. The applause grew stronger, louder. She left the stage, mingling with the crowd. Questions. Everyone had questions. People patted her on the back, stuck out their hands, pressed in all around her. Everyone wanted to touch a hero . . .

In those first few days at Walter Reed Army Medical Center, Kendra would wake for brief moments, wondering where she was before darkness would swallow her again. At one point, half-conscious, she believed she was still on the battlefield, wanting to join the fight, to be shoulder to shoulder with her battle buddies, angry that she wasn't able to stand, thinking, *I've got to get up.* She yanked on the IV in her arm and tried to pull out the tubes inserted into her throat. Doctors sedated her again.

Over the next week, she lived in a dream world.

Home—Monticello, a nothing little town tucked away in Jasper County, Georgia. One gas station. A Dairy Queen. Population, less than three-thousand. *Familiar faces*—Jerry Ray, her stepdad, an Army staff sergeant in his uniform. *Voices*— Ms. Burdge, the second-grade teacher from Jackson Elementary, calling her, "Kendra, your momma is here. She's come to get you early today."

Something about the teacher's voice had a familiar, lingering place inside Kendra's memory, or was it the day she was remembering? She was seven years old the day that Gayle, her momma, came to school and told her that her daddy, David, had left—gone with little more than the snap of a finger. Momma took her to a single-wide trailer. "We live here now," Momma had said. Kendra never again saw the inside of the house she'd lived in.

She heard the voice again, pulling her up from the depths of sleep, "Kendra, your momma is here, Kendra . . . Kendra . . ." Finally, like a swimmer pushing off from the bottom of a pool, she broke the surface, gulping a mouthful of air. She blinked her eyes, opened them as wide as she could, then squinted until blurry images came into focus. Her eyes, blackened by blood vessels ruptured in the attack, looked like black holes. She saw a nurse. Someone else behind her.

"Kendra," the nurse said again, "Your momma is here."

"Momma?"

"It's me, Kenners, I'm here," she said. "Can you see me? Are you blind?"

The look on her momma's face almost broke Kendra's heart. "I'm not blind, Momma, why'd you think that?"

"Have you seen your eyes? They're like two lumps of coal."

Kendra involuntarily touched her eyes, her face, felt the cuts and welts from bomb shrapnel, her swollen flesh, and cracked lips. "I must look pretty bad, huh momma?"

"I'm just glad you're not blind. I thought you couldn't see. Your daddy's here too."

Gayle and David, for the sake of their daughter, mended their broken truce. Frayed beyond permanent repair, it held —temporarily.

Jerry Ray, on reserve duty in Nevada, loaded his pickup. Stopping just long enough to take a break and gas up, he drove the thirty hours straight through, joining Gayle and David at Kendra's bedside.

When he walked into the ICU, Jerry Ray, a big man, took up all the space. He towered over David, stuck out his own bear claw of a hand. David took it. Jerry Ray nodded to Gayle. Their marriage had lasted long enough for Gayle to issue a "don't go or else" ultimatum when, a few years into the marriage, Jerry Ray had volunteered to go down range. Not an ultimatum kind of guy, honor bound to serve, he left Gayle. He'd stayed in Kendra's life.

Inside the ICU, he turned his attention to Kendra. Machines blinked at him. Lines from I.V. packs hanging on hooks above her head, snaked their way into her arm. Her face bruised and still swollen, made him suck in a quick breath. Jerry Ray was career military, squared away, disciplined, organized, calm in tough situations, strong—but the sight of her made him pause.

Jerry Ray stepped into her life soon after 9/11. He brought order to the chaos that was how she'd lived back then.

She grew to admire the man and the soldier that he was. His influence became indelible. Patriotism ran high in small towns like Monticello. Since the morning she sat in junior high school and watched the towers collapse, Kendra often thought about joining the Army. The way Jerry Ray carried himself helped seal the deal. Kendra enlisted. Step-father and step-daughter had become as alike as the uniforms they wore. They were soldiers.

Jerry Ray leaned in over her. Unlike anyone else in the room, he understood what it meant to be lying there, having done your duty. "Hey soldier," he said, taking her hand. "You okay?"

His hulking presence, the strength in his voice, made her feel safe. "Yes sir, I am now, now that you're here." Tears, like drops of morning dew clung to the tips of her eyelashes, then fell onto the back of Jerry Ray's hand.

When Jerry Ray finished holding her, reassuring her, reassuring himself, that she would be okay, he stepped into the shadows. Out of respect, he gave the room to David and Gayle.

———

Days later, a nurse rolled back the sheet that covered Kendra. "I've got to change the dressing," she said. Kendra turned her head away.

"Your wound looks good, soldier, no infection. Take a look."

"No ma'am," Kendra said, then closed her eyes. "I don't want to see what you're doing. I don't want to see what's left of my leg."

"Sooner or later, you'll need to," the nurse said, then finished bandaging the wound and left.

Kendra looked down the length of her body, to the hollow in the sheet where her leg should have been. "I don't want to see you, you hear me? I don't want to. They can't make me look," she said, then closed her eyes, trying to deny what her mind saw clearly, but what the soldier in her didn't want to believe.

The pivot to her physical recovery, what led her to lift and peek beneath the sheets, to look in the mirror, and to attack physical therapy and rehab, was her soldier's sense of obligation. Spurred on by the belief that she belonged with the men and women she'd left down range, determined to rejoin them, she threw herself into her recovery.

Surgeries followed. Thirteen if you didn't count the little ones, more than thirty if you did. She fought through the pain when surgeons picked metal fragments, shards of glass, splinters of wood, and bits of gravel from her flesh, and cried when they'd debride dead skin from her wound.

She masked the pain with heavy, addictive medications.

In the rehab gym at Walter Reed, sweat ran down her face, between her breasts, dripped from the tip of her nose. All she cared about was learning how to walk again. Her mind was set. She hated the wheelchair. She grimaced, pushed herself, closed her eyes, and took her first step sixteen days after arriving at Walter Reed. She badgered therapists into letting her use a walker. They marveled at her motivation. She abandoned the walker, moved to two crutches. One. A cane. And then came the day when she tossed that aside, raised her arms in the air and walked on her own. She wanted to be the first woman combat amputee to go back down range.

Six months after being blown up, Kendra knew that her life, no matter how hard she rehabbed, had rearranged itself. She'd been uncertain about the military as a career, had been leaning in that direction, but that choice had been hers to make. The Taliban had robbed her of more than part of her body. They'd ripped away her way of life. She couldn't run. Jump over a stream. Scramble up a river bank. Kick in a door. Leap into a Humvee. Dive into a bunker.

Sgt. Kendra Lou Garza couldn't ever go down range again.

But she could say goodbye to her battle buddies. In late fall, just a few months after her injury, her guys would rotate out of Afghanistan. Determined to be there to greet them, Kendra sought and received permission to fly to the United States Army Garrison Bamberg, in Germany. Soldiers deployed to and from Afghanistan from Bamberg.

"I'm going to walk on my own," she told her physical therapy team. "I'm not going to greet my battle buddies from a wheelchair. If I can't go down range with them, I'm at least going to march with them. I'm going to stand and salute them. Help me get ready."

She'd learn never to ask a physical therapist to push her again; they're only too happy to oblige. They got her ready, but not without more sweat in the workout room of Walter Reed—and not without more medication.

In Bamberg, in uniform, her Ranger beret at a jaunty angle, Kendra stood without the help of a cane. She walked under her own power. Saluted her battle buddies, Medic Flynn, First Sergeant, the rest of the team. She'd hoped to be standing on the tarmac, ready to salute them as they stepped from their airplane. She settled for seeing them two days after they landed, in time to attend the end of their redeployment ceremony.

In Monument Park, formerly Desert Storm Park, they honored Kendra by adding her name to the unit's Rock Memorial Monument. Carved out of huge gray stone, the names of all the unit's WIAs are engraved on the rock.

"I thought you were going to die on me," Flynn said. "Good thing you didn't, I'd have killed you if you did. You would have ruined my record. No KIAs."

Kendra had not seen Anthony, a soldier she had met and fallen in love with while originally stationed in Bamberg, since they'd both deployed to Afghanistan. When they'd met in Germany, they came together in a rush, the first real love for either of them. He was a handsome man, warm brown eyes, black hair, chiseled (like Kendra) from long hours in the gym. They fit together well. Same age, both good looking, both single, neither ever seriously in love before, and both in uniform.

When she was wounded, Anthony, still down range, had no idea that she'd been injured. Not a spouse or fiancé, the Army had no obligation to get word to him.

Kendra worried. *What if he sees me and doesn't want me? I'm not the Kendra who was physically strong, beautiful. I'm not the woman who could run, pump iron side by side with him. I could do anything. Now, I feel broken. I'm wearing a fake leg. Part of me is missing. The pretty part. Anthony, he's handsome, beautiful, so strong. What if, what if . . . it's one thing to be behind closed doors, take off my clothes, how do I take off my leg in front of him? How?*

In the waning months of Anthony's deployment, Kendra, walking more and more, looking more and more like the workout partner she'd been to him, found the courage to contact him. Separated by war and circumstance, they traded emails, rekindling their connection. Bit by bit, they moved past the emails and began talking again. The desire for each other that gnawed at them couldn't be denied. When his tour ended, his enlistment over, Anthony left the Army and joined Kendra in D.C. Anthony, originally from Texas, took Kendra home to San Antonio and made her his wife.

The new bride, still a long way from fully recovering from Afghanistan, met the physical therapy team at Brooke Army Medical Center. Sometime in late 2012, DOD placed her on the Temporary Disability Retired List (TDRL). She was declared unfit for military duty by reason of disability whose conditions have not stabilized sufficiently to permit the assessment of a permanent disability. More operations. More rehab. More prosthetic fittings. More pain meds.

Stories have a way of telling themselves. Real life isn't always "and they lived happily ever after." Kendra and Anthony stayed together for a couple of years, long enough to have a daughter together. Kendra and Sky, a beautiful, blonde, blue-eyed little image of her momma, went home to Monticello, back to the old single-wide trailer.

"Momma," Kendra said, after looking around the old trailer, "this place needs some work. I want to buy it from you and fix it up. This is where I want to live."

Gayle, happy to be free of the trailer, moved to nearby Conyers, still close enough to Kendra and Sky. Kendra drew up plans for the build-out of the trailer and started construction. David, her dad, took over.

Kendra boarded a runaway train. She traveled the country, speaking to Veterans' groups and charitable organizations looking to use her as a fundraising machine. Invited to a Braves game, she threw out the first pitch. Everyone, it seemed, wanted a piece of her. She smiled, told her story again, and again, and again, but standing in front of audiences brought all the heartache and loss back.

She doubted herself. She'd lost more than a leg. Confidence. She'd never believed she had a firm hold on Anthony. She'd talked herself into believing that she would have made the Army a career, telling herself that that had been ripped away too. The person everyone wanted to see on stage wasn't the person Kendra believed herself to be.

To prove it, she began to make herself look like the person she'd felt she had become. She didn't feel pretty anymore, so why pretend? She quit working out. Gained weight. The extra pounds confined her more and more to a wheel chair. She looked less and less like the woman who walked on her own when she said goodbye to her battle buddies. In an effort to numb her feelings, she began using more and more of the medications supplied by the VA. She emptied the bottles. What should have lasted a month, lasted only days. She went looking to the VA for more.

They refused.

Already an institutional addict, she became a street addict. There are a lot of misconceptions about drug addiction. Few people, if any, set out to become addicts. Kendra certainly didn't. But without really realizing what was happening to her, the years of medications had made her physically dependent. Now, that dependence had grown into an emotional craving as well. She called Anthony. "Come get Sky," she said. "I can't take care of her, not with the way I am right now."

Heroes are in high demand; but when people place you on a pedestal, there's only one place to go. Kendra fell. Hard.

The door to Kendra's remodeled home blew open, ripped from its frame. Sundered splinters of wood showered the foyer, littering the floor. Mike, her girlfriend's man, raced to the attic, just ahead of four members of the Jasper County Drug Task Force rushing into the house, guns drawn. They knew Mike. In violation of his probation, wanted on new drug charges, he wouldn't go easy.

Kendra, shocked out of a heroin high by the violence of the raid, jumped off the sofa like a startled rabbit. She stood out of the way, an unwilling spectator to Mike's losing struggle with the task force. Pulled from the attic, he continued to resist, adding to the charges he already faced.

Afraid that the task force would arrest her, too, Kendra fled. She grabbed keys to Mike's pickup, a new, jacked up, red Dodge Ram. She didn't get far. Terrified, driving wildly, half blind with fear, still high, she passed out. The truck veered onto the shoulder of the road at a high speed, toppling a utility pole, splitting it in two. The spinning truck rent the soft shoulder like a shear plow. Dirt flew in all directions. The tires blew out. The force flung Kendra, unconscious, unbelted, to the passenger side of the truck.

A passing motorist stopped. Called 911.

"911. What's your emergency?" the emergency dispatcher said, her voice a metallic monotone.

"There's been an accident on Stark Road, about five miles west of Monticello."

"Is anyone injured?"

"I think so."

"Ma'am, stay on the line with me. Police and EMS are on the way."

"Hey Deddy, where are we?" Kendra said.

"We're in the emergency room," her father David said. "Spaulding Hospital. EMS brought you here. You were in an accident."

"I don't remember much of that," Kendra said. "Was it bad?"

"You crashed some guy's truck. Totaled it. I think the docs are going to let you go. I'll take you home. You got a door that needs fixing. Police want to talk with you before we leave."

"No charges are going to be filed, Kendra," one of the members of the drug task force team said. "You were found in the passenger seat, asleep. Without witnesses, we can't prove you were driving. You want to tell us how you got there?"

"No sir. I don't really remember. I was sleeping."

"Doubt that, ma'am. I think you were driving."

"No, sir. I was asleep. I don't know who was driving."

"We know you were driving, just can't prove it. We're

going to be watching you from now on. What are you doing with a guy like Mike in your house? He's not a good guy. You gotta get yourself sorted out, you hear? You're better than this. You're free to go, then, until next time. If you don't get some help, there *will* be a next time; you know that, don't you? Get some help before something worse happens."

"Yes, sir, I will," Kendra said.

Later, at home, after her father had left, Kendra sat alone, lost, confused. She felt her world coming apart. The line that had kept her tethered to any chance at sobriety, rubbing against the rock that had become her addiction, had frayed to the breaking point. Fighting had been her way of life long before the day she almost died in Afghanistan. She'd fought then with all her strength to survive. A good soldier, a strong soldier, she'd fought to come back physically. She'd known how to fight that battle. This was different. She found herself in a battle she had no idea how to win. She had no weapon strapped to her leg. Her leg was gone. Losing the strength to fight any more, she called a new friend, a street friend. "Let's get high," she said.

She had better friends.

Members of the drug task force, some of them veterans, had meant what they said. They watched Kendra. They believed in her, knew she was better than the life she was living. More than once, they pulled her off the street, took her to rehab. She walked out the back door. They took her back. She left again—and finally, refusing to let her fall any further, they arrested her in her own home.

Tipped off that she had heroin in her home, they busted down the door, the same door that David, "Deddy," had carefully carpentered back into place.

Possession of heroin.

Possession of drug paraphernalia.

They showed up at her arraignment. They spoke against releasing her while she waited for a court date. "Your honor," one of the deputy task force members said, "She'll be back on the street, using again before the day is over."

The judge paused. The courtroom went silent. Kendra felt like she was back at COP Charkh in Afghanistan. The air suddenly heavy. Everyone holding their collective breath.

The judge looked at the task force deputies. He looked around the courtroom, then at Kendra. His chest rose and fell with the weight of his decision. He weaved his fingers together, placed his hands against his lips, whistled through his fingers. He dropped his right hand, picked up a pen, scribbled something, then raised the back of his hand to his lips, inhaled slightly, before exhaling a throat clearing "ahem."

"Based on the recommendation of the task force deputies, I'm ordering you to be held in Jasper County Detention Center to await trial."

Kendra dropped her chin to her chest. Sheriff's deputies quickly moved toward her, one on each side, grabbing hold of her arms. She felt the viselike grip before they moved her hands behind her back, clamping a set of handcuffs around her wrists.

Hours later, still handcuffed, stunned into silence, she shuffled into a grey van with several other prisoners. At the Jasper County Jail, processed, strip searched, robbed of every remaining bit of dignity, she pulled a bright pink jumpsuit with the letters JASPER COUNTY DOC on the back, up over her prosthetic, too shocked to even cry. A guard gave her a pitying look, and in that look, Kendra saw how much she had let slip away.

It was time to start over.

For the next seven months, while she waited to go to trial, Kendra, denied anything stronger than an aspirin, got clean. She started working out again, losing weight, getting in shape. She pushed herself to get free of the wheelchair she'd confined herself to while doing drugs, wanting as much as ever to stand on her own.

She worked on more than her body. She found new weapons to fight the emotional battles, those surprise attacks, ambushes that she'd never been ready for. Some of the answers she found in books. Some in counseling. Most, in the mirror. She couldn't undo the things that had happened to her. She could no longer deny the hollow beneath the sheet where her leg should have been. When she looked, it wasn't there. *It wasn't there!* It was lost; a part of her, not all of her.

She readied herself to face the judge once more.

Members of the task force team showed up at her trial. On the bench, the judge shuffled papers, looked up, did the same little throat-clearing "ahem" and looked at Kendra.

"Young lady," he said. "I have a decision to make today. So do you. It's been seven months since you last stood here. Have those seven months changed you at all?"

"Your honor," Kendra said, "those seven months saved my life."

"I'm going to give you a choice, then," he said. "There are consequences to your behavior. Do you understand that?"

"Yes, sir."

"Then I'm going to give you a choice. Twenty-seven months of court-mandated drug rehabilitation, go to school or get a job, and stay clean. Or I can sentence to you to more time in prison. Which will it be? And before you answer, understand if you slip back into old habits, you'll go to prison."

"Sir, I'd like to go to college," Kendra said.

Twenty-seven months later, men and women filed into Marshall Auditorium, the main event hall on the campus of Fort Benning. Drill sergeants, faces hidden beneath the wide brim of their traditional campaign hats, known more commonly as "Round Browns," braced and saluted officers. The officers returned the salutes.

Offstage, a media officer, a second lieutenant, shiny butter bars glistening on his collar, clipped a tiny microphone to the front of Kendra's shirt, a collared, black polo with an embroidered Purple Heart over the pocket, her name, *Sgt Kendra Lou Garza*, stitched above the emblem. "Wait here," the lieutenant said. "Someone will introduce you." Satisfied that the mic was secure, he turned and walked away, stopping at a table, center stage. He slid a chair from behind the table and positioned it to the side. A glass and a pitcher of water sat on the table. The lieutenant spun the pitcher around, the handle now an easy reach from the chair.

From her vantage point, Kendra could see the full crowd. The auditorium buzzed. The talk she prepared, her first since completing drug rehab, much of it a familiar recount of her service, now included her struggle with drugs. Maybe including all that was a mistake.

There's a room full of drill sergeants and officers out there. Geezus, they are an intimidating bunch. What will they think when I tell them I was arrested on drug charges, served time? They'll judge me. A lot of soldiers get wounded, not all of them turn to drugs. What if they see me as weak, a failure, someone who couldn't cut it? I wish . . . I don't know. I don't know. This gig is different. My story has changed. Before all the drugs, I could stand tall and proud. I'd lost my leg. I'd given a part of myself for my country. Now part of me is a recovering addict—

She jumped at the touch on her shoulder.

"Whoa, at ease, Sergeant," said a full-bird colonel looking down at her. "I didn't mean to startle you. I'm going to introduce you, then you can walk on out. You look nervous."

"Well, sir, I am nervous. I can tell you that for sure."

"You going to be okay?" he said; then without waiting for an answer, he walked out onto the stage. The soldiers in the audience jumped to attention.

"At ease," the colonel said, then began his introduction.

Kendra hesitated. The colonel beckoned. She reached center stage, stood next to the table, looked out at the audience, and began . . .

"My name is Kendra Lou. In 2010, I lost a leg in Afghanistan. The Taliban tried to kill me, they couldn't. Heroin almost did, but I wouldn't let it. That's where the rest of my story begins."

Marlene and Kylee

MY WAY

I've lived a life that's full
I traveled each and every highway
And more, much more
I did it, I did it my way.

— *FRANK SINATRA*

FORMER ARMY SERGEANT Marlene Rodriquez moves about her kitchen. She wears a black, unlettered baseball cap that hides her long black hair. Her tattooed arms, colorfully inked, contrast brightly against a white, short-sleeved T-shirt.

Weeks earlier, I'd asked if she'd allow me to tell her story, include it in a book. She agreed, but not without voicing a reserved skepticism. Now that we're talking, Zoom lets us side-step COVID, she raised the question again.

"Why would anyone want to read about me?" she asked, disappearing from my computer screen, reappearing with a mixing bowl. But as we exchange small talk while she slides a cutting board across a counter, she brings stories of her own to the conversation, stories of the upside-down world that was hers through three combat tours in Iraq.

A loud beep interrupts us. Marlene disappears from view again but I can hear her. She reappears. "That was the oven," she says, then slides scallops from the mixing bowl into a baking dish.

A cat mews, maybe it's the smell of shellfish. Steam seeps from the open oven. Marlene pushes the scallops inside, closes the oven door and sits for a minute. A short haired dog, lean, cared for, pushes her nose under Marlene's arm, nuzzles her. Marlene strokes the dog's head. She looks up from the dog, pauses, stares into the computer screen with a look that, if we were playing chess, would say, *it's your move*. Given the cue, I ask about her first deployment to Iraq.

———

On the morning of March 20th, 2003, the 46th Transportation Company, attached to the 3-6 Calvary, rolled into Iraq. Marlene was just a private back then. She had the driver's seat of one of the vehicles in the convoy, a HET, heavy equipment transporter. She piloted the monster truck out of Kuwait, lumbering behind nimbler gun trucks, Humvees, and MRAPs racing ahead through an opening in a berm on the Kuwait/Iraqi border.

American flags attached to many of the vehicles flapped wildly in the onrush of wind as the convoy sped into Iraq. Within minutes, they began taking fire. U.S. air support and ground fire engaged the Iraqis. Heavy equipment mechanics, soldiers, part of the crew traveling with Marlene, had the HET's six. They returned fire. The smell of cordite, smoke, and dust filled the cab of the HET. The Iraqis fled. They'll regroup. They'll attack again. Not always immediately. Some-times hours later. Sometimes, the next day. Always sporadic— and always with bad intention. In less than a day, vehicles become pockmarked by small-arms fire.

For several months, well after President George W. Bush's

"Mission Accomplished" declaration, Marlene, the 46th, and the 3-6 chased first Iraqis, and later insurgents, all over Iraq. They secured roadways, villages, towns, and rally points for Americans coming behind them. Large vehicles and tanks, when they become disabled by RPGs, IEDs, or small-arms fire, are loaded onto Marlene's HET. At night, the convoy "circle the wagons," the Humvees, MRAPs, trailers, flatbeds, and fuel tankers. Sometimes a disabled tank, an M1 Abrams MBT secured to the flatbed of Marlene's HET, waits for mechanics. They'll repair the tank, get it mission ready, and return it to battle.

Inside the makeshift perimeter, soldiers ate MREs, cleaned weapons, worked on their vehicles, and tried to rest. No showers. No privacy. Marlene pours a bottle of tepid water over her long black hair, soaps up, then rinses out the day. It's the best she can hope for. By the end of summer, almost six months later, some soldiers manage to get their hands on L.L. Bean portable outdoor shower bags. Marlene's crew, not that lucky, MacGyvered a water can, set it atop the HET, and for the first time in nearly six months, Marlene, surrounded by a poncho liner, a flimsy attempt at privacy, showered. It wasn't exactly private. Modesty? Forget it. But even standing in wet, muddy sand, the shower washed away what to Marlene felt like layers of dirt.

Mail rarely caught up with the roving convoy. Some of the soldiers, gone for a long time, had now been gone even longer. They reread old letters. When mail did catch up to them, it wasn't always good news. Broken promises. Not everyone back home could hold on until a soldier redeployed. But in this war, the bad news—the change of heart, the unwillingness to be alone, and everything that comes with being alone—came not only from women who abandoned promises to wait, but from men, too.

Everyone could see the heartache on the faces of those reading the bad news. Marlene had no one waiting for her, outside of immediate family. Sometimes, no letter was better than one that brought a broken promise.

At night, before dark, they secured the makeshift camp, set up guard rotations, and hunkered down. They slept, or tried to, sardined inside their vehicles. Still in full battle rattle, weapons on their laps or across their chests, soldiers closed their eyes and drifted off, only to be jolted upright by the thunder and the flashes of light from exploding artillery off on the horizon. Tracer rounds from small-arms fire tic-tack-toed the darkness.

When a fire mission ended, the artillery grew silent. Firefights paused. In the interlude, new sounds, sounds that had been muted by big noise, were gradually replaced by the threat of ominous shouts, the bounce of jostled battle gear, heavy footfalls as shadows flitted across the night, too close. Something, someone, bad guys, were always moving. On nights like that, almost every night, Marlene, unable to escape the sounds, the shadows, the threats, would abandon sleep.

Inside the vehicle, she followed light discipline. Headlamps only, and only in thirty-second intervals. No smoking. The glowing end of a cigarette, in the distance, looked the size of a softball in the dark. Marlene would glance at her watch only to discover that just ten minutes had passed. Hours to go before first light. Deprived of sleep, cheated out of a much-needed respite, she coped. They all did.

On rare occasions, without explanation, a night without gunfire, artillery, shadow, or threat surprised Marlene and all the women and men in the convoy. Marlene was always grateful for even just one of those nights. But sleep, elusive for so long, often didn't come any easier for her, even when the feeling of walking on thin ice subsided. She'd listen to the night sounds, the rest of the team asleep in the HET, their rhythmic breathing, a raspy throat-clearing cough, the chirp of crickets scraping their wings, calling for a mate, and the creak of gear straining against someone yawning or shifting in their sleep.

She enjoyed the respite, knowing that it could be erased in a hail of gunfire. Often her thoughts strayed, turned to home. The months in Iraq have taken a toll, changed her, chipped away at the paper-thin veneer that was life before she went to war. She felt the weight of her choice. She'd volunteered to deploy a month before the invasion; but even a soldier, until she is thrust into battle, isn't prepared for the everyday consequences of combat. The number of soldiers wounded— worse, killed—increased almost daily. When the convoy was attacked, her role would change from driver to warrior. She'd quickly exit the HET, go tactical, returning fire and protecting her men. She's the best shot in her team. Everyone knew it. Whenever they could, they got her into the turret of a gun truck.

Some mornings, she would stir before others, find a moment of privacy, take care of herself, then make coffee, instant, the water warmed with a heat pack from an MRE. She'd eat what she could, trying to remember what a freshly cooked breakfast smelled like. MREs are better than the average person might expect, but still no substitute for a real meal.

Each day, when camp woke, stirred, then broke down, packed up, the convoy would reform. Marlene always personally checked the load she hauled, never leaving that up to others. For almost a year, she turned the key on the HET. And every morning, the 600 HP Detroit Diesel, like a soldier with too little sleep, complained loudly, belched a cloud of oily diesel exhaust, and then, like a duty-bound soldier, answered the call, faithfully rumbling to life, carrying Marlene and her crew into the absurdity of another day in Iraq.

Christmas. Just another day for the 46th. No special meal. No ceasefire. No day off.

By New Year's, Marlene had been traversing the Iraqi

countryside for nearly a year, skirting Iraqi and Al Qaeda attacks. The days became a ruptured rhythm, fits and starts, firefights, loading, repairing, and unloading disabled vehicles, returning them to the convoy, mission ready. Even in moments of rare quiet, threat exists. Marlene is good at her job, and lucky. She's managed to stay alive.

———

Not long after the New Year, Marlene was abruptly transferred to Mannheim, Germany, a former WWII Luftwaffe airfield. Her orders, a PCS, permanent change of station, should keep her out of Iraq. Unlike temporary duty assignments, permanent change of station orders are longer-term assignments. *Years.*

Marlene's first real respite from the war in Iraq is a mixed blessing of hot showers, clean sheets, freshly cooked meals— and privacy. But her mind wanders back to Iraq. The days in Germany are full of subtle reminders, a soldier with a shrapnel-dimpled cheek, an unexplained scar, a lingering limp. She fears for the women and men left behind. For Marlene, for almost every soldier, the desire to be out of harm's way bumps up against the sense of duty to those still on the battlefield. It's a collision Marlene cannot avoid. Thinking about her battle buddies still in Iraq sends an involuntary shiver through her that not even the cold German winter can match. The chill is hard to throw off.

By April, the warmth of spring finally pushed winter aside. Sun streamed through trees. Crimson colored buds, coaxed to life, began to dot the tips of branches, casting dappled shadows on the ground. As summer approached, Marlene, inexplicably ordered back to Iraq, packed up for the start of a second tour.

———

Back in country for several months, returning from an all-night escort detail, Marlene took the passenger seat of her gun truck, an up-armored Humvee with a .50-caliber, turret-mounted machine gun. She'd given up the driver's seat to one of the team members. Her routine: drive out, see the convoy safely deposited, then, sure of the return route, she'd give the reins to one of the other team members. Their team, one of four Humvees, had safely escorted a supply convoy to its rally point. With the convoy safely ensconced, the squad of Humvees rolled back to Al Taqaddum, the FOB they operated out of. Marlene's gun truck, the first Humvee in the queue, led the way.

The sun began its climb, lighting up the dawn. Marlene's turret gunner slipped off his night vision goggles. Looking through his battle wraps, he scanned the horizon. Another team member sat behind Marlene, his M4 cradled across his lap. They were about an hour out.

Marlene's second tour in Iraq had gelled into a routine of monotonous days—supply convoys out, supply convoys safely delivered. Gun trucks herded the convoy along, bookending the lead and rear. Downtime between missions, too short. Although they needed to stay vigilant—insurgents, rogue Iraqi Army, Al Qaeda, counted on complacency—getting lost in a soldier's daydreams, lonely musings of home, was hard to fight off.

Sleep-deprived, tired, fighting to stay alert as the Humvees roll through the Iraqi countryside, Marlene mentally drifted off. It's an odd juxtaposition—the immediacy of the moment, the constant threat of attack, her responsibilities to others in the truck, against the warm, inevitable tug of memories pulling her back to home, her sister, her nieces and nephews, her parents, growing up in Colton, California, an old railroad town.

She remembers high school. She played almost every sport. Marching band, too. Trumpet. She remembers, in her senior year, the growing desire to serve, sparked by the example of her County Sheriff stepfather. After graduation, she followed in his footsteps, attended, and graduated from the Sheriff's Academy.

The path to sheriff, already narrow, required a stint as a corrections officer with no guarantee of a spot in the Sheriff's department. After almost two years with the San Bernardino Detention and Corrections Bureau, still no closer to joining the Sheriff's department, disliking the corrections officer role, Marlene abruptly quit. A few days later, she talked with a local Army Recruiter. The chance to serve, the possibility of a military career, those promises too alluring, she enlisted. Her stepfather, cautious, said, "If it's what you want, if it's what will make you happy, go for it."

The Humvee bounced over a dip in the roadway, jolting Marlene from her reverie. She looked over at her driver, twenty-year-old, Private Kevin Jones. "We good, Kevin?" she asked.

"All good, just a bump in the road," Jones replied.

Assured that it was nothing more, Marlene, turned her gaze back to the passing Iraqi landscape, drifting off again, this time remembering a conversation with her mother, before leaving for Iraq the second time. She'd talked a few times with her while stationed in Germany. Not the once-a-week conversations they had while Marlene was deployed to Korea, but more than the one conversation they'd had while Marlene rolled through Iraq during her first deployment.

She remembers the ups and downs of that first conversation, right after settling in at Mannheim. They hadn't spoken in months. They teetered on the edge of tears. The SAT-phone connection was good, clear. Long pauses punctuated the conversation. Marlene's world, the brutality of almost a year living under constant threat, wasn't for sharing. There are stories soldiers don't tell.

Maybe her mother wanted to ask, to know and understand more of what her daughter had gone through; but a mother's intuition, especially the mother of a soldier, warned her off. If Marlene wanted to talk about Iraq, she would. The conversation, awkward for the first few minutes, found its rhythm. The intimacy between mother and child, even a soldier and her mother, no matter the age, no matter how much time has passed, or the distance, is too practiced. They found their voices. While Marlene was in Germany, they talked more frequently.

Their last conversation, just days before Marlene deployed for a second time, was different. Marlene's mother, confused and angry, saddened by Marlene's sudden return to Iraq. "How can they send you back so quickly?" she asks. "It seems like you just got out of there. Can they really do that?"

"Of course, they can, it's the Army," Marlene tells her. "That's how it works."

"It makes me sad, is all. It makes me sad."

Marlene, like many soldiers, wonders what it will be like for family back home, especially her mother. Will her deployment leave behind a void? Can anyone, maybe her sister, temporarily take her place, or is she the only one who can fill that space? Will anyone miss her that much?

In the distance, Al Taqaddum comes into view. The air traffic control tower, the first silhouette to take shape, stands sentinel against the horizon. As the returning security detail gets closer, sun shimmers off the tower windows. The detail begins to slow. Drivers navigate the Humvees through staggered Jersey barriers that make up the serpentine entrance to the base. Fencing crowned with razor wire casts a pattern on the sun-bleached concrete, decorating it with a shadowed herringbone.

The detail rolled past huge mounds dotting the airbase like warts on a toad, Soviet MiG-25 Foxbat fighters and Su-25 Frogfoot fighter-bombers, buried in the sand at the command of the Iraqi dictator. Saddam knew what American pilots would do to his air force, especially since the U.S. had begun flying the F-22. His air force would get torn to shreds. He also remembered what his pilots did in the first Gulf War when sent to defend the homeland. They flew their fighters to the relative safety of Iran rather than face annihilation, and Iran never gave them back.

"Hey Rodriquez, we're back," Pvt. Jones said. "You with me?"

Marlene turned away from the window. "Yep, just daydreaming. Let's secure this vehicle and get some chow. I'm tired. I want to get some rest. We'll probably roll out again tonight."

"Yeah, you got that right."

Marlene watches him walk away. Jones is a good soldier. She knows when there is trouble, she can count on him.

———————

The days seem endless. Roll out. Roll in. Pilot a gun truck. Provide security. Switch it up. Become part of a convoy. Drive a fuel tanker, a HET, or a PLS, a Palletized Load System vehicle, the Oshkosh M1074A1.

Long hauls. Short trips.

The months pass. Daytime temperatures that routinely hit 100 degrees Fahrenheit during the summer months moderate to a comfortable 70 degrees during the day as winter approaches. But the Iraqi winter is short. By early spring there'll be no getting away from the heat or the noise of the open airfield. Black Hawks, whining airplanes, and grumbling trucks spew a fatiguing cacophony, 24/7. The caustic stench of jet fuel, not so bad during the short winter, will return with the warm temperatures.

It's then, more than ever, that soldiers welcome the refuge of their CHU, containerized housing unit, the modern-day wartime hootch. Marlene shares a CHU, an aluminum box measuring 22 x 8 feet, little bigger than a commercial shipping container, with another soldier. She has a cot, and privacy, a window, roof vent, power cabling, and air conditioning against the summer heat. The CHU she is housed in has a shared shower, nothing like the MacGyvered water-can shower of the first tour. A private toilet divides the unit into two separate sleeping quarters.

Early afternoon on Christmas Day, an early winter sun, high in the sky over Al Taqaddum, spars with a cool breeze coming down from the Euphrates River off to the north. Ripples rib the surface of Lake Habbaniyah to the south. DEFAC, the cooks in the dining facility, worked their magic, conjuring up a special Christmas Day meal. Marlene is as relaxed as she's been in weeks, but even on Christmas Day, there's work to be done. There's no ceasefire, no declared holiday truce. The day, Marlene's second consecutive Christmas in Iraq, even with the special meal, turns out to be just one more day of many. Marlene's combined deployment is on the other side of 465 days.

Tomorrow, they fall back into their routine.

By late summer, Marlene, promoted to sergeant, worries more. Not for herself. She's embraced the role of caretaker and leader for the few soldiers assigned to her. She's been trusted with their lives. She takes the responsibility seriously: in her mind, in her heart, it's a sacred obligation. She stays cautious, continuing to take the reins of whatever vehicle they rolled out in. She's more practiced, more experienced, knows it, and uses that experience to keep her soldiers safe. The young soldiers in her charge remind her of herself in the early months of her first tour. They're like her back then, raw, inexperienced, untested—until they're not.

Marlene and the soldiers she deployed with roll through

spring. By September, the end of her second tour is in sight. She could be home for Christmas.

"Let me drive out tonight, Sarge?" Private Jones asks. "I'd like to try my hand at this PLS."

"Not a chance. You know the drill. I drive out. You can drive back."

"I'll race you to the truck, Sarge. I get there first, I drive. How else will I ever learn?" Jones shouted, then took off, reaching the truck and climbing into the driver's seat before Marlene had barely moved.

As Marlene approached the truck, the night clear, stars dotting the sky, she saw the smile Jones flashed at her, his grin so wide he could've eaten a banana sideways. She thought about ordering him out. She could have. Maybe she should have, but she didn't.

Hell, maybe Jones had a point. How would he learn if she didn't give him a chance? The eagerness in his voice convinced her. She left him sitting there while she checked the load they were hauling, CHUs for another FOB, then climbed into the passenger seat. She ignored an uneasy feeling, the intuition that something bad was about to happen, something connected to her decision to let Jones drive, something that maybe could have been avoided if she'd driven out.

She looked over at Jones. He looked back.

"What, Sarge? You're not changing your mind now, are you?"

She hesitated. "Alright, Jones, let's roll," she said.

The starter motor turned, spinning loudly, its sharp outcry screaming until the monster diesel engine that powered the PLS growled to life. Gun trucks took up positions, front, rear and spaced into the convoy. They rolled out through the serpentine, belching diesel exhaust into the night sky. Fifteen minutes outside the wire, the first gun truck rolled past an Iraqi Police checkpoint. The rest of the convoy followed through. The last gun truck rolled by. The convoy cleared the wire.

A klick out from the checkpoint, a daisy chain of IEDs began exploding under and around the entire convoy. Drivers instinctually took evasive actions. The convoy separated. Gun trucks went tactical. Tracer rounds stitched a lethal crisscross pattern against the darkness. The ambush was well coordinated. Enemy spotters hiding in the dark waited until vehicles rolled over or near IEDs. When a truck entered a kill zone, the enemy spotters detonated their bombs, wired rockets and artillery rounds. Hidden behind high dirt berms that lined each side of the roadway, they rose up over the crown of the berms, unleashing a hail of small-arms fire.

The PLS, disabled by an IED, the cab blown apart, the enemy bomber's lethal timing perfect, spews fuel and oil everywhere. Marlene, dazed, riddled with shrapnel, dismounted, rushed around the front of the PLS to return fire. In the dark, she found Kevin on the ground, just outside the PLS, near the driver's door. Maybe he'd pushed the door open and tumbled out, more likely he's been blown out of the vehicle.

Marlene let go of her M4, freed both hands, rans her fingers over Kevin, searching for the wounds. Her hands are bathed in warmth. She pulled them away, raised them close to her face, trying to understand how to help him, where she can stop the bleeding, treat a wound.

I can't see in the dark. Is it blood? Oil? Hydraulic fluid? I can't tell, Kevin. I can't tell. I can't tell. I can't tell . . .

A gun truck rolled up. Hands reached out, grabbed Marlene.

"Relax Sergeant, I've got you," she hears someone say. "You're hit. Medic's got your guy. Black Hawk is incoming. We'll get you guys outta here."

The *thump, thump, thump* of the Black Hawk adds to the noise and chaos. Dust and debris swirl into the night as the Black Hawk hovers, lands. Kevin and Marlene are loaded into the helicopter. Kevin lies stretched out on the deck. Medics rip away what's left of his battle rattle, cut away the remnants of his uniform, stuff his wounds with combat gauze. Excessive blood loss is the number one killer on the battlefield. They work feverishly, inserting IV's, applying pressure, talking to Kevin, keeping him awake.

Marlene looks at him. He sees her.

"Hey, Sarge, I'm okay, really, I'm okay. I'll buy you a beer when we get back to Germany," he says. "You'll see. I'm okay."

The Blackhawk carrying Kevin and Marlene landed at Marine COB Lima, a smaller, contingency operating base, much closer than the FOB at Al Taqaddum. If the medics were going to save Kevin's life, every second mattered. COB Lima had a small CSH.

Inside the CSH, Kevin and Marlene lay side by side on litters less than a few feet apart. The Marine Corps doctors began working on the two Army soldiers. They cut off Marlene's uniform, staunched her more serious wounds, then began removing shrapnel from her arm, legs, and body, stitching the larger wounds, cauterizing others.

The right side of Kevin's body had been ripped open. Shattered bone and tattered flesh made it impossible to find the origins of multiple bleeds. Marlene listened to the doctors working on Kevin, their quick, concise orders, their life-saving directions. Marines with O-negative blood type and Kevin's blood type lined up to give blood, some of them twice, in an effort to keep him alive while surgeons cauterized and tied off veins and arteries. He bled faster than the Marines' blood could be given to him. His heart, without enough blood to keep it beating, just stopped. He died next to his sergeant, not much more than an arm's length away. Marlene listened to the doctors as they let him go.

Had she made the wrong decision? He'd teased her, wheedled her into letting him drive out, and she'd caved. She'd thought it would be alright, but alright doesn't taste this bad. Alright doesn't rise into the back of your throat to choke you. Alright doesn't leave one of your soldiers dying on a litter next to you. Alright doesn't . . .

Marlene recovered from her wounds, cuts, burns, and a concussion. Just a few weeks later, she rolled out on missions again. The rest of her tour passed quickly. Suddenly it was December, time for her to leave Iraq again.

Her last night, lying awake, she could not sleep. She stepped outside her CHU, looked up at the Iraqi sky, took a deep breath, and let herself think about Kevin Jones. She wondered about him, his future, the future denied him, and all the women and men lost.

Home for Christmas with Kevin gone, her parents divorced, was almost unbearable. Old traditions left her empty. Out of place, a stranger in once-familiar places, Marlene ached to report to her new unit, the 306th Transportation Company, Fort Carson, Colorado.

Gone for more than three years, if you counted the deployment in Korea. Time for Marlene, for all deployed solders, had stood still. In Iraq, she had pictured everything back home, family, and life in and around Colton, as it had been before she'd left on deployments. But in her absence, the world she'd known had been reordered, changed without her.

An involuntary rift, a gap that widened, that loosened the

connection to home and family, felt too wide to cross. Their worlds, so different, made conversation awkward, punctuated by long silences. Marlene, awash in a torrent of emotions, became more reticent than even her usually quiet self. There's an ache that she felt at being the one always leaving. She was, after all, the cause of her family's worries and fears; they're the ones left behind to wait and wonder about her.

What if? What if she hadn't joined the Army? Does her mother wonder who she might have become if the Army, Iraq, war, hadn't grabbed her, changed her life? Would she have a family of her own? Maybe. Maybe without the Army, she might have become a police officer in nearby L.A. There were a lot of maybes. A lot of what-ifs.

What pain would they have felt if she, and not Kevin, had been driving?

Before her leave runs out, Marlene leaves for Fort Carson. She cannot renew the connection, pull the drawstring tight on family ties. She's been too long removed from the people she used to know. They're there. She is the one gone.

Before she left for Fort Carson, Marlene visited an attorney, made out a will. "Just to be on the safe side, in case I get deployed back to Iraq," she told her mother. "I don't think I will, but if I do, you need to know now, my chances of coming back, they're not good. I've been lucky, really lucky. Sooner or later that luck is going to run out."

By late spring, Marlene, forced to break some surprising news, called her mother from Fort Carson. "They're sending me back to Iraq," she said.

"What? Again? This is the third time. How? How can this happen so quickly? How? You said you probably wouldn't have to go back. You've already been twice."

"It is quick. I even said to myself, 'Gee! Wow! Three times, three times they are sending me back, deploying me to Iraq again.' I mean I haven't been back in the States very long."

"Well, can't you do something? Can't they send someone else in your place? Why does it have to be you? You've been there twice."

"You know that's not how it works. I've told you that before," Marlene said, laughing into the phone at her mother. "I got to this new unit, the 306th, but they already had orders to deploy. I'm part of them now. I'm combat ready. So, I go. It's the Army."

Fifteen months later, after pushing fuel all over Iraq, into Turkey and Jordan, Syria too, Marlene rolled out of Q-West, the former Iraqi Airfield at Qayyarah, not far from Mosul. She's done this trip before, Q-West to a small FOB, an out-and-back daytime gig. Part of the trip runs on blacktop like Hwy. 80, some parts of the route on desolate stretches of two-lane road running through sunbaked desert. If all goes well, the trip from the American-held airfield to the nearby FOB should be a quick, safe turnaround. Back at Q-West for evening mess.

Marlene, a staff sergeant now, sat in the passenger seat of an M915, a long-haul tractor trailer used to pull large heavy fuel tankers. Her truck, with its load of fuel secured behind it, is the 6th or 7th vehicle in queue. Marlene bristles at the lack of protection, and the comms missing from her M915. They have no ICE, IED Countermeasure Equipment, a jamming system that uses low-power radio frequency energy to block radio signals that detonate enemy IEDs. Some vehicles have Q-Net, an armor system that stands off from the vehicle's surface and "catches" an RPG before it hits the outside of the vehicle itself. Hers does not.

Luck of the draw. There are not enough of these devices to go around. Marlene rolls out; her 915, just lightly up-armored, is almost naked.

Gun trucks, scout vehicles, rolled out ahead, hoping to

spot any signs of ambush ahead of the convoy. They looked for the unusual: new asphalt patches on blacktop highway, freshly turned dirt at the base of berms that line the sides of roadways.

They'd stop the convoy if they suspected signs of hidden roadside bombs, IEDs, movement on rooftops when the convoy rolls through towns or villages. The glint of sunlight shimmering off of a mirror, or worse, the worn banana magazine of an AK-47. Quiet towns—places that should be busy, but are unusually empty—pose unwelcome threat. Something as benign as a discarded soccer ball raises the hair on the back of the necks of the men and women driving or sitting on the canvas sling seat of a Humvee turret. They looked for vehicles flashing headlights, or bystanders, a lone male with an unusual appearance, a vehicle driving erratically. If there is a hidden bomb, where is the trigger man? All of these things hold potentially lethal consequence. It's a deadly game of chess. Enemy spotters, patient grandmasters, watch and wait for the Americans to make a wrong move.

By midday the convoy rallies at the remote FOB, unloads the fuel that Marlene hauls, and turns back to Q-West. They approached a small city. A mud hut village nestled into the Iraq desert on the outskirts of the city squats near an intersection that the convoy must cross. The village looks empty. A figure rose up out of the shadow of a mud hut, lifted, aimed and fired an RPG, a Queen's Gambit that buried itself into the 915, drawing everyone's attention, a distraction before a full assault.

There's no explosion.

"It's a dud," Marlene says to the private driving the 915. "A dud! How lucky—"

Her words are swallowed up in the blast of an IED that explodes beneath the cab of the 915. Marlene, flung around like a dummy, is bounced against the inside of the destroyed cab. Her body, limp, slammed against the walls and roof of the 915, ricocheting like popcorn against the lid of a kettle. Shrapnel clawed its way up Marlene's legs, reaching beneath her armor-plated vest, ripping into her body, tearing at her. By design, the tanker is unscathed; insurgents are after the fuel. The tanker is empty.

The driver's door, crushed by the blast, refused to open. Marlene jumped from the passenger side, high above the roadway. The driver, Pvt. Wootin, scrambled out behind her, screaming in pain. Insurgents unleashed a hail of gunfire. Wootin fell to the ground in front of Marlene. An AK-47 round slammed her forward. She staggered, struggled to stay upright, shot through the shoulder.

Wootin lay on the ground, screaming, face contorted with pain. Marlene ran her hands over his body, found no visible wounds. The haze of gunfire is relentless. *Not again, not again, I'm not losing another one.* Marlene draped her body over the private, shielding him, before the world around her went dark.

The gun trucks, on perfect cue, a lethal choreography, moved to protect the convoy. Within minutes, Black Hawks swooped down, driving the insurgents off. Marlene, loaded aboard a Black Hawk, faded in and out of consciousness. Medics frantically go to work, tugging off battle rattle, cutting away clothing, stemming the flow of blood from her legs, stomach and shoulder.

It's September 16, 2007, just 6 days short of two years from the day Kevin Jones died.

In Landstuhl, doctors work to save Marlene's life. Most of her vital organs, ruptured by the blast wave, have hemorrhaged. Doctors make lifesaving decisions. Vital organs are operated on, pieced back together; others, organs beyond any chance of healing, are removed. Head injuries have swelled Marlene's brain. Doctor ease Marlene into a medically induced coma, hoping to save her life.

"Can you tell me your name?" a nurse asks.

"Staff Sergeant Rodriquez, Ma'am," Marlene replied.

"Do you know how old you are?"

"That's easy, I just had a birthday on September 3rd. I'm 29."

"Where are you from?"

"California."

"That's good, Sergeant, really good. Do you remember what happened?"

"We were ambushed. What happened to my driver, the private I was with?"

"No idea. You were the only one flown in. You're lucky to be alive. Doctors will be in soon. They'll tell you more, everything that's happened to you. You've been in a coma for seven days while your brain began to heal itself. Your memory is good. That's a good sign. The rest of your recovery is really a wait-and-see, but the doctors will explain what comes next."

"Sergeant, I'm the doctor who operated on you. How are you feeling?"

"Like I've been shot, Doctor."

"Funny. There are some things I want to tell you. You were really banged up when you arrived. The blast was so close it ruptured—well, what didn't it rupture? Listen, to save your life, it was necessary to remove most of your reproductive organs, your gallbladder, too. Shrapnel ripped you up pretty good. I had to take part of your stomach and colon. Both were full of tiny pieces of shrapnel like birdshot. You'll recover, probably need to be careful about what you eat. I'm sorry, but you won't have children of your own . . ."

The doctor's words trailed off. Marlene felt a tingling in her legs. A metallic taste soured her mouth. She felt nauseous, her stomach seemed to revolt, the room blurred, she stared blankly into space. Her body went rigid, then began shaking and jerking uncontrollably. The injuries that had robbed her of a family had also rigged the normal pathways of her brain with short-circuit ambushes, attacks as random and unpredictable as hidden IEDs.

The seizure subsided—briefly. But a wave of seizures followed, rolling over her, one following another, almost as soon as each one ended. The blast wave had left her with trauma-induced epilepsy.

Weeks later, Army doctors still searching for the right cock-tail of medicines, trying to lessen the frequency and severity of Marlene's seizures, sent her back to Colorado, to Fort Carson. The seizures fought back. They controlled the high ground, baffling modern medicine, sending Marlene into uncontrol-lable fits or knocking her to the ground as often as ten times a day—ten unpredictable seizures a day.

Months passed. "You're unfit for active duty," the Army doctor said. "The seizures are not much better. You certainly cannot hold a weapon. Maybe some admin role, but you'll never deploy again. That said, you've got two options: imme-diate Medical Discharge or Convalescent Leave."

"I want a full-time Army career," Marlene said. "I'll go on medical leave."

Returning home, still unable to gain control of the some-times dozens of daily seizures, Marlene, unable to live alone, rented a home near her mother's house. The VA provided a full-time, live-in caregiver nurse.

Five years later, only a few steps closer to recovery, an Army Medical Board waved the white flag. Surrendering Marlene's hopes of getting well and resuming her career, the Army medically retired Staff Sergeant Marlene Rodriquez. Still blaming herself for the death of Kevin Jones, over-whelmed at the prospects of a future still racked with epileptic seizures, bouncing between DOD and VA care, no career, no chance to be of service, no chance at a life of independence, Marlene made a decision—a bad one.

Not long after receiving the Med Board's decision to retire her, Marlene moved quickly. Her caregiver, out on a short errand, gave her all the time she needed. She pulled a step ladder from the wall of her garage and scraped it along the floor to the center of the garage. She clamped two hands around an outdoor extension cord, snapped it taut, testing it. *It'll do.* The noose she tied, the directions found on Google, looked right. She climbed the ladder, slipped the noose over an exposed rafter, then tied off the end. She stepped back, surveying her handiwork.

Looks right. I'm tired of all of this, just tired. I just want it to end.

She climbed the ladder, slipped the noose over her head, kicked the ladder away and swung like a pendulum, forward, back. Once. Twice. *It only takes a few seconds to lose consciousness. That's what Google articles said.* The noose slipped, unraveled. Marlene, barely conscious, crashed to the floor. *Snap!* Pain jolted her fully conscious.

I'll be damned, I think I just broke my leg. This is just perfect, perfect. I'm sick. I can't get well. I let Kevin die. I was his NCO. It was my job to protect him. One job. Protect your soldiers. I failed. I can't even walk down the street without wondering if I'm going to have a seizure and fall flat on my face. I can't live alone. Now this. I try to kill myself and I break my leg? Really? I mean, really?

A smile started at the corner of her lips and spread into a grin. She chuckled, then burst into laughter, tears streaming down her face. *You gotta laugh. Who tries to kill herself and breaks a leg instead? Me, I guess. Geez, if it didn't hurt so much, it'd be really, really, funny.*

The next few days were hard. The smile that glided across her face as she sat on the floor, bewildered by the unexpected fall, had been replaced by a grimace. Her leg throbbed. While she waited out a mandatory 72-hour suicide watch, she had time to think. She missed the healthy soldier she'd been, when she could grip the high handle on the side of a HET and swing herself up off the ground in one single motion. She'd been able to run for miles, drive all night, sling an eighty-pound .50-caliber over her shoulder, climb up on top of a Humvee and lock it onto a mounted swivel.

Anger and sorrow at the death of a soldier she had responsibility for had haunted her for so long she couldn't remember what life felt like before. Kevin's life, his future, was gone. Denied. But that was the life of a soldier. Soldiers die in war, but *this?* Swinging from a rafter, that's not soldiering. Marlene knew it. And that's not how she could honor her fallen soldier, Kevin.

Something in her changed. She'd hidden behind her guilt for too long. For the first time in years, her world felt somehow different. Her anger and resentment, her hopelessness, subsided. Life was a gift. She'd been spared, given a second chance. Whatever would happen next, Marlene knew, no matter what that would be, it would need to start with her. She gave up wishing that she could go back in time; even if she could, what would she have changed? She'd loved being a soldier. She'd loved her fellow soldiers, would have given her life for any one of them—almost did. Choosing a life where she'd never have known these things? No.

The hard moment when Marlene decided that life, crippled by seizures and haunted by ghosts, wasn't worth living, had passed. The door to her life as a soldier had closed. The smoke of the battlefield had cleared. She had scars, so many, but not so many that she couldn't heal. She understood that the wound that was three-and-a-half years in Iraq would still pull at her, that her past would always be a tug of war with her future, but she could plant her heels in the ground, lean back and tug against it.

There was new terrain to navigate. She took a first step on a path to health. It wasn't easy. There were missteps along the way, but through her own research, trial and error, diet, and exercise, she first gained control over the seizures, then beat them into submission. With the unpredictability that had robbed her of confidence and independence behind her, she moved on. She took advantage of a seizure-free life, a gift to herself, and enrolled in university. Combining what she'd learned on her own with formal education, she earned a bachelor's degree in recreational therapy. She began to travel the country, speaking to others about her experiences, hoping that others might follow her down the path she'd discovered.

There are still difficult moments. Marlene doesn't always know if the peace she's found is lasting. But the question isn't so painful anymore. She's more nimble at pushing away the doubts and demons. Life in Iraq had been moment to moment. It might still be, but now Marlene lives life on her own terms.

Jennifer

NOT BY SWORD ALONE

"WITHOUT WOMEN TAKING an active role in Afghan society, rebuilding Afghanistan is going to be very difficult."

—*Khaled Hosseini*
Author of The Kite Runner

Iraq, 2007

On September 26, 2007, shortly before noon, Army Specialist Jennifer Hunt sat behind the wheel of a Humvee, the third vehicle in a small convoy of five Humvees filled with American Civil Affairs soldiers. She'd been in Iraq since late August, after almost two months of staging in Kuwait, not long after she'd graduated college and married another soldier. They deployed to Iraq together.

In Iraq, a land where friend and foe are often indistinguishable, American soldiers never knew what trouble waited outside the wire. The Iraqi army, pressed to fight another of Saddam's mother of all battles, had been crushed in 2003. Twenty-eight days after the second American invasion, Iraqi soldiers fled the battlefields, leaving behind a vacuum. By that fall, insurgents, a caustic collection of rogue Iraqis, Al-Qaeda, and ISIS fighters bent on owning Iraq, filled the void.

Four years later, a blanket of uncertainty still covered most of the country.

Iraq felt different to Jennifer, more dangerous than her year in Afghanistan. Soldiers here, more vigilant than she remembered from her time among the Afghans, stayed alert. She followed their lead—always geared up in full battle rattle, always donned her Kevlar instead of the soft bush hat or baseball cap she wore during her year in Afghanistan. She carried her M4 wherever she went. She kept a Beretta M9 strapped to her right thigh.

The small convoy approached a nearby Iraqi Police checkpoint after rolling out of FOB Falcon, the team's home base. The FOB sat a short distance outside of Baghdad proper, about 13 kilometers (8.1 miles) south of the Green Zone. One of the police guarding the checkpoint spotted the convoy and raised a gate. The convoy slowed to fifteen, maybe twenty miles per hour. The guard signaled them forward. Jennifer followed the first two Humvees, checked her mirror for the two behind her. The guard smiled, nodded, motioned her through. His arm, like the pointer on a metronome, moved back and forth, keeping time to some internal beat. She smiled back, tipped a gloved hand to the brim of her Kevlar, and continued past the guard shack, speeding up once she cleared the checkpoint.

No signs of ill intent.

The Iraqi Police checkpoint sat just outside of FOB Falcon. Good or bad, the location was a common practice. Situated in urban outskirts of Baghdad, it was also common, almost routine, for FOB Falcon to be mortared by insurgents who used the surrounding neighborhoods as cover. Insurgents reserved IED ambush for convoys and soldiers outside the wire. To remain less visible, to baffle enemy spotters waiting to trigger a roadside bomb, convoys usually moved at night.

Daylight put convoys at greater risk. But safe travel was never a guarantee, especially when Iraqi Police—bribed, or in league with insurgents, smiled, raised a gate, and waved convoys into harm's way.

Jennifer kept a safe distance from the Humvee in front of her.

Midday sunlight turned surrounding buildings into shimmering towers of light. The reflection blinded the turret gunners, drivers too. Scanning windows, doorways, and rooftops was almost impossible. Everyone squinted behind sunglasses or tinted goggles. Sun bounced off the Humvee in front of Jennifer. In the glare, she lost sight of the Humvee. Anxious, she lifted her foot from the accelerator, ready to slide her toe onto the brake pedal. A cloud passed overhead, temporarily blocking the sun. Vehicles, dulled by the shadow, appeared a safe distance in front of her. She relaxed.

Just a few klicks out from the police checkpoint, someone with ill intent waited. Silent. Invisible. He let the first vehicle pass, then the second, hoping that an attack in the center of the small convoy would inflict the most casualties.

Now, now!

A roadside bomb, a shaped charge IED, exploded. The world spun out of control. Shrapnel blew through the Humvee. Smoke spiraled up toward the clear sky.

Shelton, Connecticut, United States, 2001

By her senior year, seventeen-year-old Jennifer Baker had an inkling that helping others, understanding more of the world, traveling internationally held her interest. These things, she thought, might someday make up her life. Those desires fed her curiosity. College, she knew, would help her.

"We're all for that," her parents said. "Money might be tight, but we'll find a way."

Too young to decide on the exact direction her life would move in, Jennifer knew enough about herself to know that life held more than small-town Shelton, Connecticut. She had no inclination to join the military, never really gave it much thought, even after a plume of smoke rose high in the sky on the morning of September 11th—smoke that covered all of lower Manhattan, crossed the East River, drifted into Brooklyn and beyond to the sea.

In the weeks that followed, the more outspoken students at Shelton High School and high schools across the United States voiced their wrath. The bravado, real or exaggerated, waned quickly. For a few, anger remained. The more impulsive, those wanting revenge, joined the military. Few, if any, understood actual military life.

Jennifer, sandwiched somewhere in that stratum, had been deeply troubled by the 9/11 attacks, but revenge or a rush to enlist in the military didn't fit her reaction. There was no, *Oh my gosh, I have to join the Army*, moment for her.

By late November, weeks after the Twin Towers heaped chunks of slag, dust, and debris onto streets, buildings, cars, and people below, and just days before the fires at Ground Zero flickered and finally died, life at Shelton High School had mostly returned to normal. Students who'd rushed into the hungry arms of the Army talked about heading off to boot camp. Others, fingers crossed for early acceptances into the school of their choice, had sent off college applications.

Jennifer leafed through college brochures, huddled with the school's guidance counselors, and visited a few colleges. On a whim, she'd sent an application to the University of Hawai'i at Mānoa. She took a shot. *Hey, why not?* The university replied with regrets. Jennifer's escape plan, her getaway from harsh New England winters, disappeared.

Most days she hitched a ride home with friends. The day

that would change her life was no different. She slid from the front seat of a friend's car and leaned back in to grab her backpack.

"Thanks for the ride," she said.

"No problem. I can pick you up tomorrow, if you want."

"Okay. Thanks, that would be great, see you tomorrow."

She fit her key into the locked door and pushed her way into the empty house. She shed her backpack, turned on the light in the kitchen, and searched for an after-school snack, Hostess Twinkies, milk. Snack and drink in hand, she settled in front of the television, channel surfed, rode the wave to Comedy Central in time for the daily episode of *Whose Line is It Anyway?*

Host Drew Carey kicked the show off with his usual line, "Welcome to the show where everything's made up and the points don't matter." He bantered with the show's regulars, celebrities Colin Mochrie and Wayne Brady, then in the reverse fashion of rival show *Jeopardy*, he opened the show with a question.

"What are inappropriate things you might say when meeting the Queen of England?" he said, reading from a cue card he held.

Colin pounced, offered up his line. "I lick your stamps all the time," he blurted out.

The audience roared. Jennifer laughed out loud.

Before Wayne Brady could respond to Carey's next prompt, the kitchen telephone startled Jennifer. She made it to the phone on the third ring.

"Hello?" she said.

"Hello, this is Staff Sergeant John Simmons, from the United States Army, good afternoon, ma'am. I'd like to speak to Jennifer Baker," the sergeant said, his voice rising on a hopeful note.

"Um, this is Jennifer."

"Miss Baker, as I said, I'm Sergeant John Simmons. Let

me explain the reason for my call. I'll be visiting your school by the end of this week. I'll be meeting with individuals like yourself, mostly high school seniors. The purpose of those meetings is to provide you and some of your classmates with information about careers in the military, specifically the Army. Military service can pay for college, you know. I'd like to meet you while I'm at the school. Can we do that?"

The sergeant paused, ready to overcome any reluctance that Jennifer might voice. Most recruiting calls went that way. But not this one.

"Sure, I'll meet with you," Jennifer said. She heard what sounded like the sergeant taking in a quick breath.

"Well, I—um—ah—I mean that's outstanding Miss Baker. Outstanding!"

Before the school week ended, seventeen-year-old Jennifer Baker, without her parents' knowledge or permission, sat in the school library with two soldiers, Staff Sergeant Simmons and a younger sergeant. Neither one fit her image of a soldier. Simmons, more a Clark Kent look-alike, wore thick, black, military issue eyeglasses that partially hid a lazy right eye. As he talked the eye wandered outward toward the side of his face, then inward as if he was trying to see something on the tip of his nose. When he looked straight at Jennifer, one eye battled the other. The lower ranking sergeant, mummified, sat staring straight ahead, a vacuous smile etched on his face.

Oh wow, not what I expected.

Still, the conversation intrigued her. Simmons probed. Jennifer answered. The call and response continued. Simmons played the right notes, suggesting, once he heard that Jennifer had an interest in international relations, that a stint in the military could provide relatable experience.

"You know, I just remembered," Simmons said, "there is a specialty occupation called Civil Affairs. Civil Affairs is a liaison role in foreign countries where America might be engaged in military operations. You work with NGOs."

"NGOs?"

"Sorry, non-government organizations. As part of the US military liaison, you'd work with local officials and the people of whatever country you'd be serving in. It's a job right in line with your interests."

"It sounds exciting," Jennifer said.

"It is!" Simmons said, feeling like he'd struck a chord. "It's also a specialty that is only available in the Army Reserves."

"What does that mean?" Jennifer asked.

"It means," Simmons said, "that after boot camp you can come home and go to college."

"That sounds pretty good."

Simmons rallied for a big finish. "And besides," he reminded Jennifer, "your college will be paid for."

Later that day, after supper, Jennifer sat her parents down.

"You want to do what?" Jennifer's parents blurted out in unison.

"I want to join the Army."

"Where is this coming from?"

"I met with a recruiter."

"You did what? Where?"

"At school."

"You're seventeen. How did you meet with a recruiter without our permission?

"He came to the school and met with a lot of us. He said he didn't need your permission just to talk to me."

"And just like that you want to join?"

"Yes. It sounds like there is a job I would be interested in."

Jennifer spent the next hour explaining her meeting with Staff Sergeant Simmons, beginning with the phone call just a few days earlier, then the meeting in the school library. She talked about the Civil Affairs MOS, and explained that she'd be a Reservist, go to boot camp after graduation, then return home and start college.

"College," she quickly added, "will be paid for."

"I see."

"I need your permission, though. You have to sign for me because I'm still seventeen. Oh, and the recruiter said I might finish college without even going active duty."

Her parents might have wondered if that last bit of their daughter's argument was for her benefit or theirs. Who was she trying to convince?

"We need some time to think about it. How sure are you about this?"

"I'm pretty sure."

Not long after Thanksgiving, both parents agreed and signed the enlistment papers. Years later, they would admit that they didn't want Jennifer to go into the military, but they reasoned that their headstrong young daughter would just wait a few months until she celebrated her eighteenth birthday. After that, no longer needing their consent, she'd simply enlist.

Staff Sergeant Simmons had done his job. Jennifer graduated high school in June 2002 and left for boot camp. At Fort Leonard Wood, Missouri, drill sergeants and Hostess Twinkies caught up with Jennifer. Unaccustomed to the physical demands of basic training, she injured herself. Unable to continue, placed on light duty, she gradually recovered and "recycled" into another platoon. By December, having completed boot camp, the girl that had left home disappeared in her months at Fort Leonard. A soldier, PVT Jennifer Baker returned home for Christmas.

By spring, Jennifer completed individual training in Civil Affairs and returned home, living a Reservist's life and preparing for college in 2003. Her Reserve unit transferred to Maryland. Rather than join another unit in Connecticut, Jennifer left small-town Shelton, making the move with her unit. She enrolled in American University in Washington, DC, an easy jaunt to her unit on weekends. Everything she'd discussed with Simmons, everything she'd signed up for fell into place.

Until it didn't.

Jennifer completed the Fall semester, enrolled for Spring, took a break over the holidays, and greeted 2004 with the news that her unit would deploy to Afghanistan by the end of May. Active duty that had seemed unlikely, became a reality.

The news didn't unnerve her. Her parents felt differently.

Jennifer convinced them she'd be fine, then convinced her professors at American University to front load her exams. The university, ensconced in the nation's capital, readily accommodated military students. Jennifer finished the semester in late April. Two weeks later, she joined the rest of her unit at Fort Bragg, training up for deployment. In August, without much fanfare, she boarded a C-17 military airplane. They flew first to Canada, topped off the 28,000-gallon fuel tanks and readied the airplane for the flight across the Atlantic. Soldiers, restricted to the concourse, hoping for a quick beer, went in search of open bars. The bars, already shuttered for the night, left them thirsty.

"Ireland's gotta be better. We'll get something to drink there," soldiers assured one another. And they did, but not at bars. After midnight concourse bars on the Emerald Isle were closed.

"Look," someone said, pointing excitedly, "the gift shops are open. Let's check it out. They must have duty-free liquor."

Jennifer joined with a few other soldiers entering a gift shop. Shelves were stocked with Irish whiskeys: Midleton, Jameson, Bailey's. Liquors meant for sipping, gulped too quickly, wreaked havoc when the airplane hit turbulence on its way to Germany, the final stop before heading into Afghanistan.

Jennifer, worn out by the long hours in the air and too much of a good thing in Ireland, sacked out in the center aisle of the C-17. The 18-foot-wide cargo bay, even with pallets of the unit's gear strapped down in the middle of the airplane, left plenty of room for tired soldiers to stretch out. Jennifer became one of them. Living up to her motto "Death before discomfort," she pulled a travel pillow from her pack, propped her head up and dozed. She closed her eyes. Comforted by the rhythmic drone of the airplane's engines, she mused about her life as a soldier.

I'm ready for this. Twenty's not that young. Some of these guys are younger than me. I know my job. Deployment? No big deal. I got this. Hey, Army says go here, I line up. I go. I'm okay. Kinda cool, everyone in battle rattle. I'm mean, we trained for this. Extra time on the rifle range, learning how to drive a Humvee, map reading, calling in a fire mission, Geezus, I hope I don't ever have to do that. Radio training . . . battlefield first aid . . . I'm . . . ready . . .

Someone jostled her awake.

"Back on your seat, soldier. We're landing in Germany in fifteen minutes."

Jennifer looked up, rubbed sleep from her eyes, grabbed her pack, and strapped herself into the canvas seat. She locked her knees around the pack between her legs and leaned back against the cold metal fuselage.

Afghanistan, 2004

After just a few hours in Germany the airplane departed, finally touching down at Bagram Air Base. Jennifer's unit, the 450th Civil Affairs Battalion, in limbo for the next two weeks, pulled guard duty, rotated through typical security details, and mostly did the classic military hurry up and wait.

By early September, Jennifer and the soldiers of the 450th flew into Kandahar, stayed a few days, then rolled out to Forward Operating Base Lagman, one of several FOBs in and around the city of Qalāt, in Zabul Province. The 450th, combined with other groups—eighty soldiers in all, just four of them women—would become the area-operating

Provincial Reconstruction Team, a PRT. They left Lagman, a combat-ready tactical outpost, and set up a less threatening compound three miles to the west, next to the Mayor of Qalāt's offices. The move, a deliberate signal of friendship with an intended message, "We are here to help."

The 450th's motto: "Not by Sword Alone."

———

The PRT, its mission clear—help rebuild the structures of local government and civil society to the point where they can function on their own—tackled a wide range of tasks. Configured into eight-man PRT teams that traversed Zabul Province, they organized health clinics manned by US Army medics, also part of the eight-man PRT team. Beyond medical assistance, they evaluated villages for the build-out of a variety of new construction projects that would better the lives of villagers. To poor Afghans living in the more remote areas, the PRT provided cooking oils, rice, and wheat flour. Farmers and businesses starved for cash, supplies, or inventory, once vetted, could obtain American funding. The PRT did the vetting, processed the paperwork, and qualified legitimate requests.

Too many Afghans could not read or write. The PRT did what it could to increase the education of the locals, including construction of new schools, or refitting old buildings, turning them into classrooms.

This was the role Jennifer had trained for.

———

In the early weeks of deployment, Jennifer, too new, too young, too inexperienced, usually found herself in the position of lowest ranking member of her PRT team. She discovered that it really does roll downhill—in military parlance, everything crappy coming from the top of the chain of command rolled down to the lowest ranking member of the team. The lines between her role as a Civil Affairs soldier and the duties she was often ordered to perform, blurred. Often nothing more than a tagalong, she pulled security in full battle rattle. While officers took the lead, parleyed with village elders and tribal chieftains, she stood guard outside the Humvee.

Frequently she got tagged designated driver, wheeling a boxlike Humvee or a Toyota Hilux through populated towns or over dirt roads leading to remote villages. And—because she was a woman, Afghan men would not talk to her. Their refusal contributed to her limited role. Of course, that never stopped the Afghan men from offering marriage proposals.

Weeks passed. She learned, settled into the job, often traveling with a woman officer, Captain Hicks. The teams traveled with an interpreter. Communication, a layered process dictated by Muslim custom, demanded that the interpreter relay information through the men that the Captain and Jennifer traveled with.

A typical meet and greet, especially with the women of a village, went like this: "Tell the interpreter to ask the women if they need medical attention," the captain ordered. The soldier turned to the interpreter.

"Tell the women the captain wants to know if they need any medical attention."

The interpreter approached the women. An animated exchange ensued. The interpreter turned back to the soldier.

"The women want to know if the husbands of these women soldiers know where they are," he said.

The soldier informed the captain.

"What's that got to do with my question?"

The interpreter would go back, try again, turn to the soldier once more. The captain waited.

"Well?" she asked.

"Ma'am, they want to know if you and the specialist are married?"

"Great."

Other times, more often than anyone might have imagined, the men of a village, elders or prominent members of the village, would rush the interpreter. They'd point to Jennifer. Red hair a novelty. The interpreter would shake his head. The man, animated, would gesture forcefully.

"What's going on?" the captain or Jennifer asked.

"He wants to marry you or the captain," the interpreter would reply. "He has gifts, a dress, he can offer more."

The offers would be politely declined by men on the team, avoiding insult. Outside the wire, the PRT team members looked out for women soldiers. Things inside the compound, seventy-six men, four women, were different. Jennifer would get propositioned frequently. The women captains not so much. Rank does have its privilege. Jennifer was careful. She understood that one-on-one prolonged conversations with men, even as little as five minutes, could send the wrong message.

Village elders or chiefs were eager to accept anything the Americans had to offer, particularly since it almost always meant help in the form of cash. A girls' school in Qalāt, a well-attended school, needed supplies. The PRT helped. Later, the school was used as a polling place for elections. The PRT provided security. Hamid Karzai won the election.

By late November, Jennifer and Captain Hicks rolled out with a team escorted by regular Army. The PRT teams traveled in their Toyota Hiluxes. The escort providing security rode in up-armored Humvees. Jennifer looked forward to the mission. An Army veterinarian, compliments of the United States, intended to inoculate the villagers' herds, especially sheep and goats. The mission, planned for two, possibly three days, also included a medical clinic. Captain Hicks and Jennifer stationed themselves in the women's medical tent. The PRT had women doctors and women interpreters.

Jennifer saw diseases she didn't know existed.

Inside the medical tent, a woman looking for help removed her burka. She revealed a side of her face that looked mummified. The doctor, Captain Hicks, and Jennifer, too, tried to suppress their shock. They couldn't.

Jennifer let out an audible gasp, almost jumping back, her eyes wide.

"Does it hurt?" the doctor asked. The interpreter translated.

"No," the woman said.

"Can you feel anything?"

"No. I have no feeling at all."

The doctor looked at Jennifer, Captain Hicks. They shrugged their shoulders.

"I can't do anything with this. Hell, I don't have any idea what it is," the doctor said. "Whatever it is, it needs surgery, or debriding, or skin grafts. It's not anything that I'm touching, and it's not anything that can be done in Afghanistan."

The doctor spoke to the woman through the interpreter.

"We don't know how to help you," she said. "Do you feel sick? Are you in pain?"

"No," the woman said.

"Then it's best to just leave it alone."

Not long afterward, Jennifer rolled out with a PRT, the only woman member of the team. The mission, a support role on behalf of an infantry unit, required a search of women in several villages, women suspected of hiding signaling devices or detonators underneath their burkas. Only another woman could search an Afghan woman.

The team followed the infantry unit all over a mountain-side for two days. Jennifer had her own tent. Relieving herself in private became a ridiculous endeavor. She tried cutting a plastic bottle. Dumb. Tried standing up. Not cool. She finally decided that finding the most private area she could worked as well as it was going to. So, in the lexicon of the modern-day American woman soldier who fought in

Iraq and Afghanistan, she secluded herself, and "popped a squat."

If it bothers somebody, what are they going to do, send me to Afghanistan?

Deployments in combat zones have an ebb and flow, a rhythm that develops on the ground in real time. A rhythm that soldiers know. The PRTs found a rhythm. To appear more friendly, they wore baseball caps instead of a Kevlar. They rolled out in pickup trucks instead of Humvees and MRAPs. They coordinated with combat commanders to minimize impact to civilians. They were in Afghanistan to help. They made it known, and for the most part it worked. That was what they'd hoped to accomplish. That was what they hoped to leave behind.

By mid-summer 2005, the 450th Civil Affairs Battalion redeployed. But the world is not a perfect place. The 450th, the PRTs, Jennifer, and her fellow civil affairs soldiers, had done their jobs, but in Afghanistan there would always be unfinished business.

Iraq, September 25, 2007

Dust and the smell of burning rubber, charred wire, and hot metal filled the Humvee that Jennifer had been driving. Smoke overcrowded the inside of the cab. Shrapnel that had blown through the Humvee danced wildly, looking for partners. Shards bit into Jennifer's arms, a wrist, her face, burned her neck. Hot steel pierced her cheek, its white-hot point running along her jawline, tearing through flesh just below her chin. Blood, not as bad as it looked, covered her face, dripped down the front of her vest.

A larger bomb fragment gnawed at the turret gunner's leg.

Almost deafened by the blast wave, Jennifer struggled to

make sense of the shouting all around her. Mouths opened. Silent shouts. Everything happened like a silent movie. Soldiers pointed, gestured wildly. Jennifer slowed the Humvee to a crawl, then stopped. Stunned by the blast wave, the unfolding chaos, her mind worked overtime.

Process. Use your training. Who's yelling? What? What's that soldier shouting? Go? Go where? Get out of the kill zone? Of course. Damnit, of course. I got it. Roger that. I'm moving. I'm going. I'm going! No bad guys shooting at us now. No secondary attack. How the hell did this happen so close to the checkpoint? We just passed it. C'mon, nobody could plant a bomb this close without the police seeing them. A spotter. Someone in that guard shack had to see him. Had to. A payoff, I'll bet. If not, then it's police in league with the bombers. Can't worry about that now. My gunner is hurt. I need to get to Al. Oh geezus, it's bad. I need to stop, get the medical kit. It's behind me, passenger seat, behind the headrest. Okay. I gotta stop the Humvee. Out. Move. What? Who the hell has got me? Why are you putting me in another Humvee? Leave me alone. I've gotta help Al. Bleeding? I know he's bleeding—What? I'm bleeding? Nothing hurts. In shock. I don't think so. No. Maybe. Al, I need to get to Al. Where are you taking us? Back to base, into the CSH? Okay—makes sense. Stay awake. Of course, I'll stay awake. Sing? Just keep singing? What? Anything. Okay. Ever hear the song that never ends, goes like this:

> *This is the song that never ends.*
> *Yes it goes on and on, my friend.*
> *Some people started singing it*
> *Not knowing what it was,*
> *and they continued singing it*
> *forever just because…*

Inside the CSH, medics triaged the wounded. All the soldiers in Jennifer's Humvee sustained wounds. Al, who should have lost his leg but didn't, was stabilized and flown to Germany, to the Army Medical Center at Landstuhl.

Shrapnel tried, but couldn't sever his leg, his thigh as big and thick as most soldiers' chests.

The medics cut off Jennifer's uniform, exposing her wounds: burns to the neck and back of her head, shrapnel to her side, a wrist, both arms, and to her face. They started cleaning the wounds, picking most of the shrapnel from her flesh. To her relief, the wounds were not deep. She'd have a scar on her face, small, a second dimple. Nerves in her wrist, more likely bruised, possibly nicked by shrapnel, made her hand useless for several days. A headache from a slight concussion disappeared quickly. The obligatory internal exam ruled out any organ damage and internal bleeding.

Dismissed from the CSH, given large men's military boxershorts, a man's uniform, and plenty of pain meds, Jennifer made her way back to her quarters. Within a week, once again battle ready, she returned to full duty.

Seventeen-year-old Jennifer Baker had been a girl eager for life. What she found as a young soldier was a surprise. She hadn't set out to fight. She wanted to help. She did. In Afghanistan, as a member of a PRT, she helped build schools, increased literacy, encouraged cooperation between local officials and the American Military. She assisted in the development of health clinics and helped encourage women in more remote villages to seek medical treatment.

She tried to do some of the same in Iraq.

After her second deployment, after Iraq, she returned to a quiet life, children, graduate school, a career with the Department of Veterans Affairs, and a good marriage.

Jennifer and Diana solved the riddle of love.

Twenty years have passed. Bits of old shrapnel sometimes poke through her skin, reminders of war. We've left Afghanistan, Iraq, too. Jennifer and others like her, American soldiers, many of them women, left something of themselves behind—the good that they tried to do. They sacrificed, not just for America, but for people around the world.

America has a short memory. Time passes and we forget, feel safe too soon. We need people to serve in our military. Sergeant First Class Jennifer Hunt, and thousands of reservists like her, continue to serve, ready to deploy if the country asks.

Mary Jessie and her children

PSALM 23

Even though I walk
through the valley of the shadow of death,
I will fear no evil,
for you are with me.

—Psalm 23, A Psalm of David

SERGEANT MARY JESSIE HERRERA, all five-foot, two-inches of her, long, black hair held captive beneath a Kevlar, sat on a canvas sling inside the turret of an up-armored Humvee, lead vehicle in a convoy that rolled out of Fallujah. Hours earlier, the five-vehicle convoy she was part of—four Humvees and a canvas-covered M35A3, the military's workhorse two-and-a-half-ton cargo truck—had delivered several EPWs, high level Al-Qaeda bad guys, to a holding compound at Fallujah. Mission completed, they were on their way back to Ramadi, a small FOB serving as their base of operations.

During the eight months she'd been in Iraq, beginning with the American invasion in March 2003, Mary and the squad she was part of had done this run hundreds of times. They looked forward to it, considered it a good run. Fallujah, a big FOB, had perks—most notably a Chow Hall. The squad could get real meals. They looked forward to the break from MREs. For Mary, the trip meant even more. Fallujah afforded her the chance to visit with her brother-in-law, Peter, a soldier stationed at Fallujah.

When the convoy arrived, she found him working on a vehicle in the motor transport compound. They embraced. Peter smiled. "You look good," he said, "usual trip?"

"Yep, dropping off some bad guys."

They talked about everything, nothing—all the real and imaginary things they'd do once they were redeployed, once they returned state side. Like all soldiers, they missed home. Mary wanted more than anything to twist the throttle of her dirt bike. Peter missed his wife.

The reminiscing over, the visit shorter than usual, they made their goodbyes. "I gotta get back to the team," Mary said. "I'll see you next trip."

"Be safe," her brother-in-law said, embracing her, holding her, squeezing just a little tighter than usual, concern swimming in his eyes.

With the prisoner transfer complete, vehicles refueled, Mary and the squad mounted up. The trip back to Ramadi, without incident, would take less than an hour. Mary's Humvee had the lead position. A second Humvee followed. Two more Humvees bookended the convoy, the cargo truck sandwiched in between.

Mary, like most MPs, was usually tagged to drive—an assignment she didn't like. When Corporal Prieto, a much taller soldier assigned to the turret gunner position, hinted at switching places, she eagerly agreed. His six-foot, two-inch frame, a huge silhouette in the turret, made him an easy target. Mary, almost a foot shorter, wouldn't be nearly as exposed.

She loaded up the turret. Strong enough to do it alone, she mounted a 70lb, two-man carry, MK19 machine gun grenade launcher. She positioned an M249 SAW, tucked her M4 rifle within reach, and tapped the Beretta 9mm strapped to her thigh, reassured by the touch. She wore an Interceptor vest, replacing the relic she'd been wearing, a leftover flak jacket from the Vietnam War.

Mary loved rolling out on missions. She thrived on the excitement, the adrenaline rush, the fear that heightened her senses. Her instincts are primal. She can see, smell, taste trouble. In the instant before an attack, in that suspended space before actual engagement, she saw everything in slow motion. The world around her would go silent. Each time, in the split second before all hell would break loose, she felt a lurch in her stomach, something unlike anything she'd ever felt before. Everyone would bolt into action, each soldier playing a part, partners in a dance, the choreography lethal. Everyone knew the steps. Mary's as good or better than any of her male counter parts. She knew it, so did the rest of the team. She was a trusted figure in the gun turret.

Haunted by a recurring dream, Mary forced herself to stay alert. In the dream, her dead uncle, a Vietnam Veteran, young, tanned, handsome, "Shorty" everyone called him, sat on a cargo pallet near a C-130 airplane on a sunbaked runway, not in Vietnam, but here in Iraq. His story— wounded in Vietnam a half century earlier, awarded a Purple Heart and a Bronze Star—is threaded with Mary's. They're both part of a family with a history of military service, a sense of obligation instilled in them by their parents and grandparents, a legacy knit into the fabric of their lives.

The day, overcast, an ominous grey, sent a chill through her. Getting comfortable in the turret felt impossible. She tried to find her rhythm, rocking a bit on the sling, scanning the horizon, standing to relieve the butt-numbing pressure of the canvas sling. She listened to radio chatter. Nothing clicked.

Little things bothered her, the weather, the conversation with her brother-in-law shorter than usual, the worried look on his face when he'd told her to stay safe. She forced herself to check everything again.

I'm not on my A game. Snap out of it, Herrera, get it together.

The weather felt cold, colder than it should have been. Clouds, bloated with the threat of rain, loomed above the convoy. She's afraid, not for herself, but for a possible attack, the *what ifs*. What if she missed signs of an ambush, or enemy spotters? What if her weapons jammed? What ifs. There were always a lot of them. One of the things about Iraq—there's a surprise in every box of cereal.

It's a dangerous run once they leave Fallujah, navigate a few connecting roads, and pick up Highway 1—a route criss-crossed with kill zones, hidden bad guys, ambushes and assaults. The trip from Ramadi to Fallujah and back is the same lethal absurdity on every roll out, over and over, a continuous loop, a playback of a bad movie. Rogue Iraqis, Al-Qaeda linked insurgents, ISIS, Ba'ath loyalists, every insurgent with a martyr's wish, waited.

"Patience and gratitude are the way to happiness," the Muslims say.

Go for it, Mary thought.

Insurgents buried IEDs in the road, or at the base of tall dirt berms bordering the roadway. They'd watch, silent, hidden in the shadows or along a route the convoy had to traverse, their patience rewarded when a convoy entered a kill zone. Then—*boom!* They'd detonate a bomb, follow with a small arms ambush or, damage done, they'd disappear.

Mary remembered the dream.

Her uncle, talking with a bunch of guys, turned to her. Dog tags dangled from his neck. In the dream he wore jungle boots, scuffed and dusty, the leather lined with scars, a faded green T-shirt, and the baggy, olive-green jungle fatigues all the Nam guys wore.

But he's real time. He's here in Iraq. How can that be?

He's young, just like every picture Mary has seen of him from Vietnam. In the dream, he turned away from the other guys. His eyes locked onto Mary. She returned the stare, watched him beckon to her, motion her forward. She walked over to him. "Uncle Shorty," she said, "what are you doing here?"

"I'm just watching over you, kid," he said, "that's all. You're going to be alright. Don't be scared. You're going to be alright."

The last time she had the dream, just days earlier, she found a SAT phone and called her mom.

"Mom," she said. "I had a dream about Uncle Shorty."

"Really?" Mom replied. "Okay, so?"

"Yeah, it's nothing, I guess. Right?"

But they both felt something was off. Mary said goodbye.

In another hour a darkening sky would steal her light. But if everything went okay they should be back in Ramadi before dark. Until then the convoy is prey, hunted as they roll back to base. In the turret, Mary scanned the horizon, hoping to find the hunters before the hunters found the convoy. She glanced down at the soldiers inside the Humvee then lifted her head and peered into the highway in front of her.

If they're out there, I need to put eyes on them first.

Over the eight months of her deployment, war, combat, and everything that went with it seeped into Mary, wicked its way from the soles of her feet into the pit of her stomach, through her chest and into her heart. The adrenaline junkie in her craved action. Danger awakened something in her, something unexplainable, but she couldn't escape the weight of loss; no one could. Life teetered on the brink. They'd leave the FOB at Ramadi, roll out on a mission, and come back later in the day carrying the bodies of guys who were shot up—blown up. Soldiers she'd eaten chow with in the morning died by lunch time.

Not today. Everybody eats chow tonight, everybody.

The convoy rolled toward a bridge, one they had to cross. The Humvee dipped into a small hollow before a slight rise in the highway. For an instant, Mary lost sight of the bridge until the Humvee crested the incline. Her eyes struggled to adjust to the late afternoon shadows. She squinted, swallowed hard, a foreboding caught in the back of her throat. For eight months, she had bent the odds in her favor. Which way would they bend today?

She squinted harder, peered through her glasses, read the shadows, translated the veiled images: two silhouettes, tall figures inked against the sky stood near the bridge. The convoy was closing the distance quickly. Her breathing quickened. Her chest rose and fell like a bellows, pushing her warm breath against the cold air, the vapor whisked away in the rush of oncoming wind.

What's coming should be unimaginable, but it's not—at least not for Mary and the squad. What's coming has come at them too many times to count. She saw everything clearly. Two men. Her eyes settled on them. One raised an arm, stretched it in front of his chest, cupped something in his hand. He raised his other hand, poked a finger at whatever he had cupped in the other. She saw other figures scrabbling from beneath the bridge, ants scrambling for a crumb, ready to swarm and devour.

Guessing game over. Cell phone. Bad guys, a lot of them. Ambush. This is going to have a bad ending. This day doesn't belong to anything good; I knew it when we rolled out. I knew it.

Until now, Mary had always felt protected. Maybe that

was her mother's intent when she named her Mary Jessie. Mary, the mother of God. Jessie, a trade-off for Jesus, because if her mother had another boy, she wanted to name him, Jesus. Mary Jessie—protected by those she is named after.

She radioed to the men inside the Humvee. "Two bad guys on the bridge, more coming. Cell phone. Punching in numbers. We're gonna get hit. Get ready, it looks like a full ambush."

After more firefights than she could count, pulling the trigger still did not come easy. It didn't matter if she hit someone or not. She intended to. In her mind that was the same. It's the job of a soldier. It's something she has to do, hopes she won't, but will if she must. It never got easier.

Adrenaline coursed through her body. A single second of alarm gave way to reflex. Zero to warrior in an instant. She pushed the MK19 to the side, raised the SAW, a lighter weapon, its range much farther, more maneuverable, a better weapon against a small-arms assault.

She aimed, began firing, engaged the enemy. She felt something smack her upper arm, a feeling as if someone had pelted her with a rock—hard. Her arm jerked upward. She winced, almost let go of the trigger, then gripped again, tighter. *Oh, it's just a rock. Someone hit me with a rock. Keep your focus, Herrera.* She aimed again and kept firing. A crimson stain blossomed from the hole in the sleeve of her uniform.

Brass rained down from the turret, littering the inside of the Humvee. Smoke escaped through open windows. The smell from gunfire, hot brass, spent ammo, caustic, seared the inside of everyone's noses, mouths, eyes. The bark of weapons, a deafening din echoed against the inside of the cab.

She laid down a suppressing fire until her fingers refused to obey, rendered useless by a second round that blasted through her forearm. Bone and flesh exploded. Her fingers slipped from the pistol grip of the SAW. Her arm, held captive inside the sleeve of her uniform, dropped down to her waist.

She tried to lift her arm, find the trigger. *Not a chance!* The first round, what she thought had been a rock, had passed through her upper arm, breaking bone on the way. The second bullet nearly tore the rest of her arm off, it fell to her waist, a gossamer thread of flesh kept it attached—barely.

Bullets bounced off the Humvee like a hailstorm before a tornado, tattooing her turret shield. IED's began to detonate all around the convoy. She tried to make herself small, tried to burrow into the turret tunnel. Her arm. She could feel it tearing away.

Oh God, I just lost my arm. It's hanging inside my sleeve. I should take a look. No! I don't want to see. No!

Everyone was mic'ed up, wearing headsets that spoke to all members in the truck, but no one hears Mary yelling into her comm. She kicked Sergeant Karl, the vehicle commander, in the back of the head. He turned, anger on his face disappearing, chased away by a look of surprise. Mary knew that look, knew that whatever he's looking at—it ain't good. "Herrera, get down, get inside!" he shouted.

Her right arm hung useless, a shattered vine tangled in the wreck of a tattered uniform sleeve, fingers trapped inside a blood-filled glove. She gripped the SAW with her left hand. *Don't you dare let it go. Don't you dare.* Fearful it would fly off the Humvee, land on the road and eventually fall into enemy hands, she clung to it like a desert viper sinking its fangs into prey.

She should've pointed the SAW toward the sky and let it fall down the turret. She didn't. Someone needed to secure it. What had protected her an instant earlier, now a too-long stick in a too-short portal, kept her stuck in the turret. Bullets etched the Humvee, scratching out her death warrant. She looked at Sergeant Karl. Confusion spread across her face. His too.

He shouted again, "Herrera, get your ass down!"

"I can't get inside. I can't let go of the SAW."

Sergeant Karl stopped the Humvee just long enough to change places with Prieto. "Drive," Karl shouted. "Drive before they daisy chain us. Drive!"

Sergeant Karl looked at Mary, lojacked by the SAW and her stubborn refusal to let it go. He climbed as far as he could into the turret, reached up and freed the SAW from Mary's grip. He lowered her to a lieutenant, an infantry officer recovering from wounds a month old, a tag-along in the back seat on his way back to Ramadi.

Back at Fallujah, Peter listened to the attack over a radio capturing the battle. He heard the explosion, the gunfire, the shouts and commands. He heard everything, including the report that Mary was a casualty. "A KIA, my little sister is a KIA? No! No! I don't believe it. I've got to get to her." He couldn't, not yet anyway, but when he did, it was against orders. He didn't care.

The lieutenant, Lieutenant Ray, laid Mary over his legs. "Hold on soldier, I've got you. Hold on," he said. He tugged off her glove, then looked at the shredded sleeve of her uniform, at the tattered mess that was once her arm. He frantically searched for a direct bleed, looked to apply pressure, hoping to slow the bleeding. *Where can I fasten a tourniquet? So much blood. Holy Christ, so much blood.*

Bad guys, the advantage of surprise gone, their damage done, disappeared like wraiths into the surrounding landscape. The Humvee raced to Ramadi, the small CSH there closer than a return to Fallujah. Mary was the only soldier hit. Bleeding out, at peace with whatever would come next, her eyes suddenly heavy, Mary sunk deep into herself. Her eyes fluttered. She blinked at everything around her. "I'm so tired. Sleepy. It's okay," she told herself, then closed her eyes and let go.

Some little girls play with dolls. Mary, as early as age seven, played with G.I. Joe figures. They fed her imagination. She staged mock battles, dreamed of leading men, of adventure, s becoming like G.I. Joe. She played with boys—cousins, neighbors. She'd play for hours. She'd create some grand battle plan, win against the odds, stand on an imaginary hill, and wave a tattered American flag.

As she grew older, the call to arms slept. By the time Mary became a high school student, becoming a soldier wasn't as pressing. Dirt bikes, a few beers with friends out on the dunes outside of Yuma, and getting through school with good grades filled her life.

Senior year arrived without much fanfare. On a whim she took a class: The Vietnam Experience. It woke the sleeping giant. The teacher introduced a cadre of Vietnam veterans, ushered them in and out of the classroom throughout the course. They told their stories, renewed Mary's drowsy interest in the military, aroused her passion.

Alea iacta est.

The influences went deeper. *La Familia.* Mary was part of a close knit, proud family, immigrants who came to America from Mexico decades before she was born. A family that had worked hard. A family that had become American citizens despite the difficulty. But most of all Mary had been born into a family that believed in God and service to the country they had adopted, a country that over decades had become their home.

"Mary," her grandmother had said, "I came here from Mexico, but this is our country. Appreciate what you have, find a way to serve this country."

"I will," Mary said.

And so, still in high school, underage, she sat her parents down, told them what she'd decided. She wanted to become a soldier. "We won't stop you from going, but we won't sign for you either. Wait until after high school," they said.

The Army had time to wait for Mary, all the time in the world to wait and welcome her like an old friend into their ranks. After a semester of college on her own, not long after she turned nineteen, still eager for a life in the military, Mary enlisted in the Arizona National Guard's Green to Gold program. A gold pair of first lieutenant bars, "Butter Bars," would be hers after college and OCS.

September 11, 2001, 8:46 a.m.

Watching everything unfold on television, Mary flew into a rage. "You don't come into my house, kill my brothers and sisters and not expect me to want to fight. I'm pissed," she shouted, at anyone who'd listen. She was—literally—fighting mad. She tried to go active duty immediately after the attacks on the Twin Towers and the Pentagon. She wanted to avenge the heroes of Flight 93.

Mary tried to explain her request for active duty to her superiors. "I take my country very seriously, this is very personal. You don't mess with my brothers and sisters and not expect payback. I want to go active now. I want to fight."

But she had a contract. The Army wanted her to finish college and earn a commission. That plan, for now, worked for the Army, and despite her eagerness to go active, the Army stuck to its guns. Semesters slid by. One. Another.

President Bush built his case for a second invasion of Iraq. On February 5th, 2003, Secretary of State Colin Powell delivered his plea for support to invade Iraq to the United Nations. "How much longer," he said, "are we willing to put up with Iraq's noncompliance before we, as a council, we, as the United Nations, say: 'Enough. Enough.' The gravity of this moment is matched by the gravity of the threat that Iraq's weapons of mass destruction pose to the world."

The Army activated Mary's Guard unit. Plans changed. The Army needed to fill its active-duty ranks.

The day she'd enlisted, long before she went active duty, her father gave her his advice. "If this is what you want, to be a soldier, if you're going to play in a sandbox with men, then you'd better meet their standards. But don't forget that you are a woman. There's a line, it's a clear line, don't cross it. Don't let your guard down and start acting like you're one of the guys. That will get out of hand quickly and you'll find yourself in more trouble than you can handle."

Turned out he'd been right. Men, Mary learned, were pretty raunchy. They fart, belch, unzip and urinate anywhere in front of anyone, including her. And mostly, all they talk about is having sex. It wasn't her world, she knew it, never played along. She didn't laugh at their jokes or acknowledge any attempt at anything more than soldierly comradeship. Anything more, she knew, was a green light for bad behavior. She understood after training with men what Dad had warned her about. It never became a problem.

Then, ready to board a bus, rally and fly off on deployment, unable to tell her parents where she was going, she wasn't sure herself, it was classified, her father added guidance to his earlier piece of advice. He pulled Mary aside. "You see those men and women you're getting on that bus with?"

"I do."

"Then remember this. They are your family now."

Her mother, not so concerned with giving her daughter advice, more worried about where she was going, worked out a code, a way around the classified location of the unit's deployment.

"Psalm 23," she said.

"What about it?" Mary said.

"If they're sending you to Iraq, just call me and say, Psalm 23. I'll know where you are going. If you can't call, send me a letter."

Mary arrived in Iraq just ten days before the invasion. The rush to war, the frantic deployment of her unit, the 855th MP

Company, Arizona National Guard, so quick that they arrived in Kuwait, the staging point for invasion, without their equipment. Even their battle-ready Humvees and the weapons they'd need to roll into an invasion—into full combat—were on ships that wouldn't catch up to the 855th for more than a month after the invasion began.

When the 855th had flown into Kuwait, landing at one of the US Army airbases, they flew in on commercial airplanes. Not long after the airplane touched down, they disembarked, formed up on the tarmac. The flight attendants, mostly women, the last to leave the airplane, empty and silent now, walked toward the airbase terminal. Small overnight bags hung from their shoulders. They laughed, jostled each other as they moved past Mary and the 855th.

A siren, its low growl building to an ear-piercing wail, screamed a warning. Scud missiles rained down on the airbase. The soldiers scrambled into bunkers. The flight attendants, panicked, crying, and screaming, crouched down on the tarmac. They covered their heads with their overnight bags. *Good luck with that*, Mary thought as she watched flight attendants flatten themselves on the ground.

Soldiers, accustomed to the attacks—more harassing than lethal—raised weapons, locked and loaded, ran toward their stations. Those who had it donned MOPP gear. Those who knew the locations piled into bunkers. The 855th looked for cover. No need. The attack, over almost as soon as it had begun, fizzled. Mary looked at the flight attendants—shaken. She felt sorry for them. They were just civilians.

As soon as she knew they were invading Iraq, part of the invasion force of March 20, 2003, Mary found a SAT phone and called her mother.

"Psalm 23, Mom. Psalm 23."

"Okay. You'll be okay."

"I know, Mom. I know."

On the day of the invasion, her unit boarded converted

school buses, the windows painted black, the buses Army tan. A few of the soldiers Mary had deployed with hitched rides with other units. Waiting until after dark, the 855th crossed into Iraq, rolling into the battle with nothing more than their Alpha Packs, obsolete flak jackets from the Vietnam War, their M4 long guns, Beretta 9mm pistols, and just 240 rounds of ammunition.

Firefights. Artillery rounds exploding. Tracer rounds buzzing back and forth—and the 855th rolled into Iraq in unarmed, unarmored buses.

During her first month in Iraq, the collapse of the Iraqi Army happened faster than even President Bush had hoped for. Saddam's mother of all wars never materialized. Neither did the WMDs. But the rapid collapse, faster than a speeding bullet, left Americans scrambling to corral EPWs. The 855th, attached to the 3rd Infantry, a mounted unit, roved all over Iraq. They were nomads following herds of surrendering Iraqis. They built temporary prisons, packed them with EPWs, and moved on to other locations. Staying mobile kept them from digging in at a permanent FOB. Most FOBs, even smaller ones, had a reasonably secure perimeter, a mess tent, and a shower trailer. On FOBs, soldiers slept in tents. FOBs had latrines.

The biggest issue for women stuck in a jarring Humvee bouncing around a war-torn countryside was relieving themselves. If one of the guys had to go, they pulled the Humvee over, stood next to the door, unzipped, wrote in the sand, and in two minutes the Humvee was rolling.

Mary, the only women in her squad, had to tap her male counterpart on the shoulder. "Gotta go," she'd whisper into her mic. All heads would turn in her direction. The Humvee would stop. Everyone except the turret gunner would leave the

Humvee. The team would set up a security perimeter. Turret gunner took the twelve and three. The driver stayed behind the open door. He'd rest his M4 over the rolled-down window, taking the nine. Mary would find a spot near the vehicle's five. Another soldier had the six. They turned away. Mary would shed her battle rattle and drop half her uniform while the patrol waited for her to finish. In the summer heat, she'd sweat so much, it was almost impossible to get her gear back on. She hated asking. She hated stopping, embarrassing herself—and so she quit asking, refusing to give in to nature's call for hours. The result: multiple UTIs.

Showers? Forget about it. Rationed two bottles of water a day for hygiene—just two, even basic cleanliness became a joke. Some soldiers got smart, sent letters home asking for baby wipes. When they got them, they enjoyed a baby wipe shower. The soldiers that didn't have them dealt with the dirt and sweat. Mary had baby wipes.

At night, without the luxury of returning to a FOB, the convoy would rendezvous at a rally point, form a perimeter with vehicles, do the things soldiers do—clean weapons, wolf down MREs, try to take care of themselves, their vehicles, and get some sleep. So much of war is the mundane, the boredom of routine, and the compromise to normalcy.

In the morning, it was on the road again.

Lieutenant Ray slapped Mary. "Stay awake! Hold your arm."

"I can't feel my arm."

"Then keep your eyes open, you hear me? Keep your eyes open."

Mary felt a flush of heat radiate through her shoulders and across her chest, the sensation comforting, warm as it moved through her body. Her legs felt a thousand tiny pin pricks. She looked up through the turret. Sergeant Karl looked down at her. She looked past him. The sky, grey just moments earlier, looked blue.

A calm washed over her. No pain. No sound.

I guess this is it. Hey God, I'm ready. It's okay. God, I'm thankful. God, thank you for letting me serve my country. If I'm dying, then this is how it should be, serving my country.

She raised her head, blinked, then closed her eyes and inhaled deeply. The scent of roses, the breath of angels some say, overwhelmed her. Someone shook her. *Don't do that. I just want to be with God. I just want to go home to him. Let me go.*

She argued with herself.

You're being selfish.

What?

You're being selfish. Think of your parents.

But I just want to let go—to go home, wherever home is when you die.

You're not going to put up even a little fight?

I'm tired.

You're ungrateful. People love you.

But everything is so peaceful, can't I just slip away?

And let your parents feel the pain of losing another child? One wasn't enough?

Okay. Okay.

Hey God, can we wait a second? I think I should change my mind. Listen, if You need me, okay then, I'm ready to go, no problem. I won't fight you on it, but if you can spare my mom and dad the pain of losing another child, then please keep me around a little longer.

Her eyes fluttered open.

"Ah, there you are," Lieutenant Ray said, "you're back. Hold on a little longer, we are almost at the CSH." Mary looked up at the lieutenant. She felt no pain, knew it was coming, knew that the swarm of bees buzzing beneath her skin would come alive. She hoped she'd pass out first.

"Keep your eyes on me, soldier. We're rolling up on the gate."

A sentry at Ramadi watched the Humvee speed toward the main gate. He raised his weapon, drew a bead on Prieto, the soldier who'd traded places with Mary. Prieto had no time to follow re-entry protocols. Mary, bleeding out, didn't have ten minutes to give. Prieto could not stop, go through a serpentine slowly, dismount, and get inspected. He yelled at the sentry. The sentry yelled back, pointed his weapon. Prieto skidded to a stop. Lieutenant Ray kicked open the door. The sentry looked at Mary.

"Go! Go! Go!" he yelled.

Medics pulled Mary out of the Humvee, laid her on a stretcher. Half the men at Ramadi lined the path to the CSH, waiting for Mary. Prieto, who'd earlier switched places with Mary, leaned over the stretcher.

"Herrera, I'm sorry man. I'm sorry I asked you to switch places," he said.

Mary looked up at him. She could see the sorrow splashed across his face. It bothered her that he thought her injuries might be his fault. Inside the CSH medics began triage. Mary protested when they began to cut away her newly acquired Interceptor vest. "Don't cut it off. Somebody else can use it. C'mon, we just got these. Don't wreck it."

The med team ignored her. The vest lay at their feet. They cut off her uniform, pushed IVs into her good arm. A tourniquet above the triceps stopped the bleeding. With the uniform gone, the full extent of the damage made the medics gasp. The round that blasted through flesh had splintered bone, too. What remained, a flimsy thread of skin, the finest silken strand, was keeping her arm attached.

The medics at Ramadi stabilized Mary, stopped the bleeding, kept her alive. She survived the moment. Her arm looked like scrap to be tossed away. Medics cocooned her arm, wrapped it in gauze and bandages, a temporary fix that held the pulpy, bloody, mess together. If Mary's arm was to be salvaged, she'd need more medical attention than she could get in country. Certain that she'd survive the moment, they carried her to a waiting Black Hawk that ferried her back to Fallujah.

The Army flew Mary to Germany, to the Landstuhl Regional Medical Center. Doctors examined her, decided to amputate. They waited a day to let Mary gain some strength.

In the meantime, Mary, one of the few women wounded in the early months of the war, became something of a curiosity. Her room filled with top military brass, even two senators. A Marine Corps general stepped into the room, made Mary an honorary Marine. *OOH RAH!*

One of the officers asked Mary if she'd spoken to her parents. "No sir, I have not," Mary said.

"Let's change that, soldier."

"Yes sir."

While officers talked to her, the call to her parents went through. Everyone gawked at her as she was given the phone, her mom on the other end of the line. Up until this point, Mary had displayed a stoicism beyond anyone's expectations. She wasn't certain she'd keep her cool once she heard her mother's voice. *Geezus, it's not enough to make me call my parents, but they're all just going to stand there and listen?*

And suddenly she heard her mother's voice.

"Mary?"

"It's me, Mom. I've been wounded," Mary said. "They're going to amputate my arm."

"I know."

"I guess I'm okay with it. I mean it is what it is, Mom, right?"

"It is. Yes. But you'll be fine. You'll figure it all out, do just fine."

"I know, Mom. I know," she said, holding herself together.

When her dad got on the phone, her steely will began to fade. Tears welled up, spilled over and ran down her face. Her lower lip quivered. She said a quick hello, told her dad she was fine, then knowing she couldn't hold it together, she said she had to go, and quickly hung up.

After talking to her mom, Mary made peace with the idea of losing her arm. The emotional ups and downs settled into acceptance. While the room still swarmed with officers, other VIPs, doctors needed to do some work on her arm.

"I've got to take this wrap off," one of the doctors told her. "We need to get what's left of your arm prepped for surgery. I've got to get the gauze off, debride the wound, wash it out. I'm not going to kid you soldier. It's going to hurt."

"How bad?"

"Well, getting that gauze off—think stripping layers of wallpaper from a hundred-year-old house."

"That sounds bad."

"It is."

She looked around the room. "They're all staying?"

"Looks like it."

"Then cover my face. I don't want them to see me crying."

"We can do that. Nurse?"

One of the nurses took the cue. She covered Mary's face with a small towel, but not before she drew a smiley face on the towel. The doctors went to work. Mary cried. The smiley face stared down the officers.

Mary couldn't see the faces of the officers in the room. Maybe some of them wrinkled their noses, the price they might have paid for their curiosity. The smell of decaying flesh rose from Mary's exposed arm like something a dog would have rolled in.

The next morning, Mary was wheeled into surgery. She'd said her prayers, accepted that she'd wake up with just one arm, but God, fate, just plain old-fashioned good luck intervened. One of the Army's best orthopedic trauma surgeons, head of the Brooke Army Medical Center's (BAMC) trauma surgical unit, had deployed to Landstuhl with his entire surgical team.

He stopped the planned amputation.

"Do a wash out again. Wrap her up. Put her arm in an external fixator," he ordered. "Let's get her to the States as soon as we can. Let's see what we can do for her once we have her there."

Mary did a double take. "So, they're not going to amputate?" she said.

"Not yet. Not here. I think he wants to try and save your arm. I think he'll try, once you're at BAMC."

———

Mary's mother stood outside her daughter's room. She wiped away her tears. "I'm ready now. I want to see my daughter." A nurse ushered her into the room. If Mary's appearance shocked her, she kept that to herself. She walked to her daughter's bed. Stoic.

"So, you made it back."

"Yeah, I did, Mom. I did."

"Well, everything happens for a reason. God has a plan for you. You know that, right?"

"I know, Mom. I know."

"Yeah," she said, a smile spreading across her face, "but you're not cool enough to know what that is yet."

Her dad stood nearby. When she looked up at him, Mary let go of the tears she'd been holding back.

———

A lot can happen in seventeen hours. It's the time limit on Ironman Triathlons. The flight time from Los Angeles to Ho Chi Minh City. It's almost enough time to thaw a frozen fruitcake. Not enough time to tan a deer hide.

Surgeons worried over Mary's arm for seventeen hours.

First, they stabilized her upper arm, repaired her damaged

biceps muscle, the triceps too. They inserted a flat piece of metal made of titanium. The plate fit on the surface of Mary's fractured humerus, the bone broken by the AK-47 bullet. Screws were placed through the holes in the plate to hold it to the bone.

Small nubs of bone, the remaining pieces of the ulna and radius allowed the surgeons to attach a cadaver bone, recreating a lower arm. They carefully pulled what flesh remained, grafted more, and wrapped the donor bone. She'd still have to fight off infection, endure dozens more surgeries, and months of physical therapy, but the Army saved her arm. Her life.

With time and more cosmetic surgeries, Mary's arm looked good, good enough to forget that it was more cosmetic than functional. She got a reminder soon enough. She'd met many injured soldiers while she recovered at BAMC. She made friends with one, motorcycles the link in the chain that connected them. While they both continued recovery and physical therapy at BAMC, they ventured into town. They visited a motorcycle dealership. They were excited. They had the money to get new dirt bikes.

Reality check.

Mary didn't, and never again would have the mobility to freely extend her arm to the motorcycle handlebar. Even if she could, she didn't have the strength to grip the throttle. Her newfound friend, missing an eye, did not have much depth perception or peripheral vision. Neither of them would straddle a dirt bike again.

After visiting the dirt bike dealership, Mary knew that she'd never be who she was before the Army, before being shot. That life was over. Her life *had* really changed. She had more surgeries ahead of her, more physical therapy that would teach her to do everything with her left hand. She had more time at BAMC, time to remember her mother's words. *Everything happens for a reason. God has a plan for you, but you're not cool enough to know what that is.* Those words hadn't haunted Mary, but they did remind her that there was a lot of life in front of her.

She could have died in Iraq.

She could make the injury to her arm an excuse or leave that part of her life on the battlefield.

She didn't die.

Doctors saved her life.

Doctors connected shattered bone, torn flesh and muscle to new bone, to good flesh, and to strong muscle. They made the pieces work together. And that's what Mary would do with her life. She'd made the pieces of her past, a life nearly lost, an arm almost ripped away from her shoulder, a career in the military denied by two Al-Qaeda bullets—she took those broken pieces, made them work together, connected them to two beautiful children of her own, education and a career, and made the pieces work together.

The Army medically retired Sergeant Mary J. Herrera. She started the rest of her life. It's a good life.

Mary continues to serve our country and our veterans as part of the staff of the Coalition to Salute America's Heroes and Building Homes for Heroes. Her story and her example so inspired others, the state of Arizona passed a bill authorizing tuition waiver scholarships to National Guardsmen and women who received a Purple Heart or were medically discharged due to injuries while serving in the military after September 11, 2001. The bill is affectionately known as the Mary Herrera Bill.

Connie in the gunner turret, ready for a convoy security mission from Turkey to Mosul, Iraq

Men and women of the 101st MP company, sleeping side by side during a break in the action in Mosul

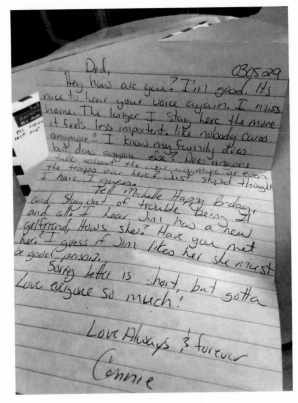

Letter from Connie to her dad, John Neill, asking about home

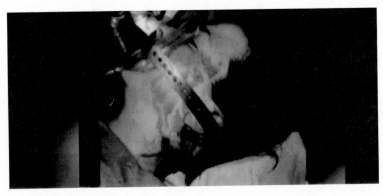

Connie being prepped for surgery after the IED blast to remove shrapnel
from her neck, Mosul, 2004

*Connie accepting a guitar from Heart Strings for Heroes, a nonprofit
that helps veterans find healing through music*

*Connie and staff at South Dakota State University, during a Purple Heart ceremony
making SDSU the 9th Purple Heart Campus in the nation*

*Connie on her horse Ara, riding trails at Fort Sisseton Historic State Park,
South Dakota*

Kendra conducting a Traffic Control Point on Route New York in Charkh,
Afghanistan

Kendra pulling guard duty watching for enemy fire and possible
VBIEDS. (She often made a peace sign in pictures so her family
would know which soldier was her.)

Kendra posing with local children at a compound her team had cleared, looking for a high-value target. Her MRAP was blown up leaving the compound.

Washing her hair with bottled water at her combat outpost, COP Charkh

Kendra (right) and the only three other women at her COP, after competing as a team in a brigade-wide competition and coming in first place in the obstacle course

Kendra on a combat flight to FOB Shank, on first arriving in Afghanistan

Kendra and her daughter Sky

Marlene resting on a Humvee's .50-cal machine gun during the invasion of Iraq

Marlene standing in front of her M915 tractor trailer in 2007, preparing for a mission in Iraq

Marlene's head is bandaged to keep drainage tubes in place as she recovers in 2008

Marlene in 2018, graduating from Texas State University with a bachelor's degree in recreation

Engagement photo of Marlene and Lakeisha, 2021

Marlene's best friend Kylee

Jennifer posing with a truck full of interdicted opium

Jennifer waiting to reenlist in style, seated on one of Saddam Hussein's thrones in Al Faw Palace

Jennifer receiving the Purple Heart Medal at Camp Falcon, Iraq

Mary Jessie and her children

*Vivian Chiu with her father, Kung-Ming Chiu, at her graduation from the United
States Military Academy, West Point, 2005*

Vivian saying farewell to her husband Jonathan as she was departing Kandahar Air Field for FOB Spin Boldak, Kandahar Province, circa 2010. He remained at Kandahar Air Field for the first half of their deployment.

Jon's arrival at FOB Spin Boldak for a short visit. Vivian's First Sergeant insisted on driving the little green "gator" so that Vivian could pick her husband up from the air field.

Vivian saying farewell to Jon again, before he headed back north to Kandahar Air Field—some 3 weeks before Vivian's injury

Vivian (wearing sunglasses) providing aid to a teammate injured after the child suicide bomber attack at the Wesh-Chaman Border Crossing at the AFPAK border

Reporting for duty!

Maggie graduating from Basic Training

Maggie in her dress blues

Maggie and her wife Mia

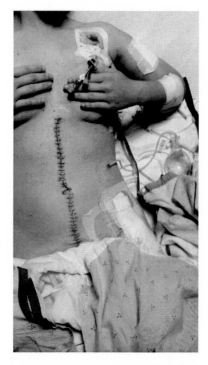

Maggie at Walter Reed, being closed up for the first time

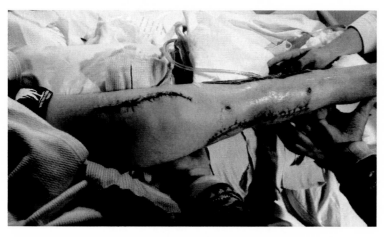

*Maggie's leg after doctors removed her fixation rods and repaired the shattered femur
with plates and screws*

Maggie's battle buddy, one of her best friends, returning home from his deployment

Maggie at a reunion with other soldiers who were medevaced out from the same blast, as they welcome home the soldiers they left behind in Afghanistan

Tara in South Korea, 2003

At the Basic Non-Commissioned Officers Course, Ft. Leonard Wood, MO

Tara and her unit taking a break during a Field Training Exercise, preparing for deployment to Iraq

Tara's vehicle after the attack—Tara was sitting in the front passenger seat

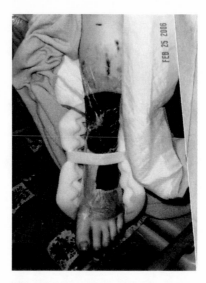

Tara's leg where her boot melted against her skin

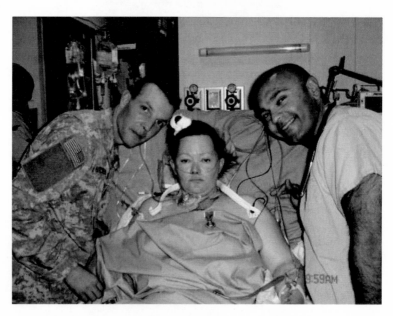

Recovering in Baghdad, with her surgeon and ex-husband

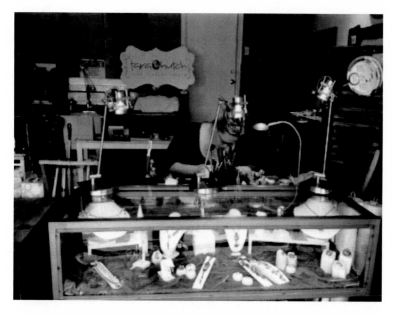

Tara crafting fine jewelry

Tara navigating an obstacle course, at a retreat run by the Travis Mills Foundation

Tara being presented with her motortrike

Tara riding her trike in San Antonio

Surfing in Long Island

*Lana on a mission with the Afghan National Army to hunt down
weapons caches, in the remote ruins of northwest Afghanistan*

*Well after midnight, waiting with friends from the 100-442 Infantry Battalion to
head out for yet another raid in the towns north of Baghdad*

On a long and hot day, Lana going house to house hunting down those responsible for the latest string of roadside bombings

Lana's Humvee, after a multi-vehicle crash with a jingle truck that left several dead and Lana's foot broken

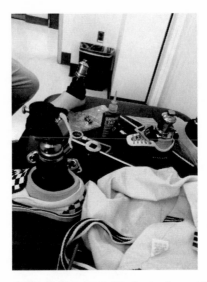

Putting together Lana's rock-climbing foot, her first specialized attachment after the foot was finally amputated in 2019

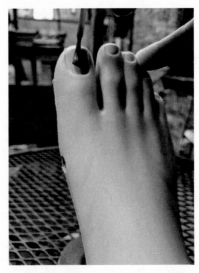

"I mean, you still gotta paint the toes in the summer…"

Lana's cat Ruby insists on chewing on the prosthetics!

Vivian and Jon

TOGETHER THEY SERVE

Duty. Honor. Country.

—Motto of the U.S. Military Academy

AFGHANISTAN. January 19, 2011. Wesh-Chaman crossing on the Afghanistan-Pakistan border. Approximately 0900 hours, AFT.

Captain Vivian Chiu, West Point, 2005, sensed movement. A shadow quickly became a small boy dressed in yellow, a boy some of the team would later say they had seen before. His yellow tunic hung over a vest strapped across his thin frame. A kufi, a Muslim prayer hat, circled his head just above his ears, exposing close-cropped black hair. His worth in the world— the number of Americans he could kill.

The boy remembered what he'd been told. *The Americans are coming. Wait for them. When you see them, you must do what needs to be done. Run to them. Run among them. When you are close, send them to hell.*

Captain Chiu looked at the boy. She dismissed him— young, small, harmless—just a kid. But he was quick to do what was demanded of him. He ran at the Americans. As he neared them, the boy pressed his thumb against a detonator wired to the vest, but something went horribly wrong. In their haste, those who would send the boy to kill the Americans had draped a flawed weapon over the boy's shoulders, fastening it against his chest so that the vest imploded.

His tattered flesh and shattered bone lay scattered in front of the American soldiers.

Later that day, a battlefield brigade officer headquartered at Spin Boldak went in search of Vivian. He'd been informed about the attack, knew that Captain Chiu was the wife of one of his officers, West Point graduate Captain Jon Cochran. He used his personal cell, called a fellow officer at Kandahar who located Jon. When he connected with Jon, the commander found Vivian.

"I've got Jon on a cell," he said. "Talk to him." Vivian looked at the phone, then the commander. She shrugged her shoulders, raised her hands in front of her chest, fingers spread apart.

"It's your husband, Captain. Take the phone," the commander said. "You with me?"

"Yes sir.

"Then take the phone."

"Jon?"

"Hon, it's me. Are you okay? What happened . . . what happened?" he slowly repeated, his voice shaky and faint.

Vivian could hear the fear as he spoke. He couldn't hide how frightened he'd been for her.

"We got ambushed. A boy suicide bomber. A boy. The vest he had on had to be made wrong, worn incorrectly, something wasn't right, otherwise he would have killed us, all of us. There was blood everywhere."

"Did any of it hit you?"

"No, I don't think so."

"Any. . . parts of him?

"I'm not sure what you're asking."

"Did any," he asked, almost stuttering, "did the boy's flesh get on you?"

"No, No, I'm sure of it."

"You sure you're, okay?" Jon repeated.

"I'm okay. I love you, Jon."

"I love you, too."

After the call, adrenaline that had sustained Vivian, that had kept her going, lessened. Pain began to take hold. Every joint and muscle seemed to beg for relief. A headache built behind burning eyes. Disoriented, she leaned against the CHU. In that instant, coming down from the battlefield high, hearing her husband's voice, Vivian understood how lucky she'd been, how lucky they'd all been. Sometimes on the battlefield luck is all that keeps a soldier alive, a dud RPG, sun glinting a warning from a worn rifle barrel, small-arms fire that misses, a shadow, a subtle warning—*an inside-out suicide vest.*

The next morning, January 20th, Army FOB Spin Boldak, near the Wesh-Chaman crossing. Approximately 0300–0700 hours, AFT.

Sometime in the middle of the night, Vivian rushed from her bed, vomiting into a waste basket until she felt as if she'd been turned inside out. The physical and emotional trauma, the horror of the attack at Wesh-Chaman, a slithering saw-scaled viper in search of prey, had found her. Disoriented, her body shaking uncontrollably, dizzy, she stumbled out of her quarters. In the dark, like a punch-drunk boxer, she weaved her way to the medical tent.

"I need help, something's wrong," she said.

Medics helped her to an exam table, laid her down, began to examine her. She'd been in the path of the blast wave. She'd been wounded in the attack at Wesh-Chaman, but not all wounds bleed. *Concussed.* The symptoms were all there, but there was more. The horror of the boy's death, imprinted in the flash drive of her memory, had already been downloaded. Some said the boy might have been a teenager. To Vivian, he looked to be no more than ten years old. She shook her head, tried to delete the image, but she didn't have a password to the file.

Small. So small. Who would strap a suicide vest to a small boy? Was he a stunted castaway, a motherless child? How? How does a child become a throwaway, an expendable killing tool to be used and tossed aside?

While the medics worked on her, Vivian began sobbing, her frayed nerves the result of the concussion. She began repeating over and over, "He was just a boy. He was just a boy, just a boy, just . . . a boy."

Unable to console her, uncertain of what to do, her shaking growing worse, medics summoned the base chaplain. The horror of the attack, the sight of her wounded colleagues, the young bomber's horrific death, her own physical trauma, Vivian had sailed into the perfect storm. The medics and the chaplain would need to bring her to calmer seas.

Reluctant to prescribe meds that might help her sleep, but confident that she'd be okay once the shaking had subsided, the medical team released her. The prescription: "Get some rest." A soldier escorted her back to her CHU. Exhausted, her body finally surrendered. She drifted off.

By early morning, deep in a dream-filled world, she heard a pounding, a distant thunder, growing louder, more insistent, pulling her from the deep sleep that had finally overwhelmed her. Groggy, she stumbled to the door, pushed it open. Her face, pinched with pain, relaxed when she saw her husband.

Captain Jon Cochran stood in the opening, silhouetted in

the morning sun. Relief shone in his eyes. He grabbed her, held her close, she pressed herself into him. The fierceness of his embrace took her breath away. She sank into his arms, stayed silent. Nothing needed to be said. She was safe in his embrace. When she did free herself, she looked at Jon. She broke the silence.

"You came," she said. "How did you get here so quickly?"

"Black Hawk. After we spoke yesterday, I had to get here. I had to see you. Are you okay?"

"Yes, I think so. It's been a bad night."

"What happened? What were you doing outside the wire?"

Vivian shuddered, looked away. "Come inside," she said.

In the dim light of her small quarters, Vivian described the attack to her husband.

She began slowly, explaining what she remembered, revisiting yesterday's events. Blood and bone, footprints left behind in the clearing, all of it was still there. Rain and wind would take weeks to erase the reminders from the ground, but the memory of the attack was fresh in Vivian's mind.

Jon listened to his wife.

By the time the mild months of the Afghan autumn had passed, a late-summer Ramadan and the annual Hajj had come to an end. Taliban on pilgrimage returned to the battlefield. Winter with its cruel cold had claimed the days and nights of the early new year. The Americans and Coalition forces limited their activities, staying inside the wire as nighttime temperatures dropped to minus 30° Celsius (-22° F).

Hampered by the extreme weather, Americans curbed patrols to mission-critical only. Taliban, free of their holy days and emboldened by the Americans' absence in the face of the bitter winter, showed their strength to locals. They increased

the frequency and intensity of ambushes and suicide bombings. And they sought targets of opportunity.

Vivian, part of a team dispatched by the 525th
Surveillance Brigade, had been ordered to survey a site at the
Wesh-Chaman border crossing and determine its suitability
for the build-out of a new biometric scanning facility. American military, cautioned to remain inside the wire unless a
mission was deemed critical, determined the site survey as a
critical mission.

Thousands of Pakistanis and Afghanis crossed into and
out of Afghanistan at the Wesh-Chaman Border every day.
The scanning facility would process the identification of those
thousands of men, women, and children. To deter insurgents,
the facility needed to be built and become operational.

Someone above Vivian's pay grade must have done a risk
analysis. The decision, despite warnings of an ambush, sent
Vivian and a team of intelligence officers and soldiers into
harm's way. They rolled out of the FOB at Spin Boldak and
headed to the nearby Wesh-Chaman border facility.

The team checked in with the American garrison
stationed at Wesh-Chaman. There to defend it, the American
troops discouraged any overt Taliban activity. Vivian's team
dismounted, secured the MRAPs and Humvees, and left the
safety of the garrison. They spread out, fell into a spaced,
staggered formation. A few locals walked with the American
soldiers.

There weren't any alternate routes to the clearing. Barriers
and smaller buildings formed a path that funneled the team
into the clearing. Some of the team members talked with
Afghan locals as the team passed through a narrow opening
and into the clearing. Locals mingling with the patrol talked to
some of the soldiers as they moved into the clearing. They
seemed friendly enough, animated, gesturing, pointing.

Taliban spotters could not believe their good fortune. The
patrol was a surprise, a welcome target of opportunity, one

not to be passed up. They acted quickly, strapped a suicide vest to the small boy and sent him on his martyr's errand.

———

"We were exposed," she told Jon. "We were in the middle of the clearing we'd been sent to reconnoiter. No one thought much of the few locals walking with us. When the kid came at us, there was no place to run to, no place to take cover fast enough."

Jon continued to listen.

———

The blast had knocked her back. She stumbled. Soldiers lay on the ground, some seriously wounded. Shrapnel rained down on the patrol—so did the boy's flesh and blood. She saw soldiers raise weapons, point at the edges of the clearing. Attacks almost always followed an ambush. The soldiers pulled their own wounded toward a concrete barrier. The bomb blast temporarily deafened Vivian. Soldiers moved like wraiths through the dust of the blast. Shouts became nothing more than faint echoes to Vivian's battered ears. Someone mouthed what looked like the words, "Take cover!"

Strange. The boy got so close to us. We should all be dead. What happened? No time for that now.

Vivian raised her M4, scanned. Gunfire erupted briefly. American? Taliban? No one knew for certain. She took cover beside other soldiers crowded behind the barrier. She checked herself. No bleeding. She hadn't been hit. Shrapnel may have rained down on her, but it was inconsequential. The blast had nearly knocked her off her feet, almost rendering her unconscious, but no open wounds. A local who'd been walking with the Americans, an Afghan man, crouched down beside her, cowering, eyes wide.

Vivian looked at him. "Are you okay?" she asked, barely able to hear herself or the man's reply. "Are—you—okay?" she said again, this time looking directly into the man's face, speaking more slowly, almost mouthing the words. "Stay down," she said, gesturing with the palm of her hand facing down. The Afghan man slowly nodded, crouching even lower, hands covering his ears, elbows pinched together in front of his face. Terrified.

The sporadic gunfire subsided. A warrant officer, part of the American team, half ran, half shuffled toward her. His shuffle turned into a limp. Vivian's head began to clear. Sound returned. The officer was bleeding. Vivian and the other soldiers pulled back to the safety of a building at the edge of the clearing. The building, manned by members of the American garrison, offered safe haven.

Two, maybe three members of the team had serious injuries, including the warrant officer. Inside the temporary safe house, Vivian began treating the injured officer. She laid him down, elevated his leg, placed his foot on her shoulder. Another soldier cut the officer's pant leg open, exposing the wound. Vivian began applying pressure to slow the bleeding. They bandaged the wound.

Vehicle commanders made it back to the Humvees and MRAPs, the mine-resistant ambush-protected vehicles that had begun to be used alongside more recognizable Humvees. Members of the team loaded the wounded. The team evacuated the area, racing back to nearby Spin Boldak.

Inside an MRAP, Vivian collapsed into a seat. Adrenaline ebbed. Her shoulders dropped. She felt dazed, disoriented. Soldiers helped the wounded officer into the vehicle and pulled themselves inside, too. An Afghan interpreter sat in another seat, staring straight ahead. No one spoke. Almost everyone felt lucky, surprised. How had the bomber come so close to the team?

He detonated the lethal vest within feet of the Americans,

yet no one had been killed. The blast had seemed contained, almost as if the vest had imploded, sucking air and debris into itself instead of blowing the American soldiers apart, leveling them like a house of cards.

The injured warrant officer broke through the silence. "I need some help here," he said, calmly. His voice brought everyone back to the moment. Vivian shook off the cobwebs. The officer seemed to be in more pain. He looked worse than a moment ago. Vivian slipped out of the seat, kneeled near him, saw the blood stain spreading on his other leg. She slit the pant leg, ripped it open and revealed the wound.

The officer's wounds didn't look life-threatening, but bleeding wounds could be deceiving. Vivian knew any soldier could bleed out in as little as five minutes. Stopping the bleeding would keep the officer alive. Inside her individual first aid kit, an IFAK, she'd packed a one-handed tourniquet, trauma bandages, combat gauze, adhesive tape, and surgical gloves. The gauze and bandages could make the difference in the officer's condition. She sprinkled anti-coagulant over the wound, applied the gauze, then tied a torn piece of his pant leg around the wound. The bleeding stopped.

Their interpreter sat in one of the six seats. He stared straight ahead. His pale skin, shallow breathing told Vivian he was in shock. She'd need to get to him, too.

Minutes passed. The returning convoy entered the gate at Spin Boldak. They rolled straight to the CSH where medics waited to unload the wounded. Soldiers like Vivian, others in the team who didn't appear to be wounded, milled about outside the CSH, collecting themselves.

The company first sergeant approached the returning team.

"I'll need that M4, Ma'am," the first sergeant said.

"What's that, First Sergeant?" Vivian said.

"Ma'am, it's SOP. Any weapon, all parts of your gear, even your uniform and boots, Ma'am, if they have blood or, ah, maybe parts of, well Ma'am, parts of a body, all that has to be surrendered, turned in. I'll say again, Ma'am, I need that M4."

Vivian held the warrant officer's M4. The weapon, slick with blood and the flesh of the boy bomber, had been entrusted to her by the wounded officer. She worried that the weapon would be lost.

"There's a chain of custody, Ma'am. The weapon will be secure. We'll get it back to the W-2, not to worry. I'm going to need those gloves you're wearing, too."

Vivian looked at her gloves, aviator gloves, the soft cape-skin palms slippery with blood, the brushed leather uppers, stained with dark brown blotches. The gloves were old friends. She'd worn them through her full fifteen-month tour in Iraq.

"They'll be lost, First Sergeant."

"Ma'am, they'll be thrown away, probably incinerated."

Vivian handed over the gloves. The first sergeant ordered other soldiers to collect any tainted gear. The soldiers started cleaning blood from boots, helped wipe blood from the hands and faces of the soldiers in the team. Everyone began removing pieces of bloodied uniforms.

Once the bloody gear was removed, bagged, secured, Vivian and the rest of the team were triaged into the CSH. Individual evaluations revealed that every member of the team had most likely suffered mild-to-severe traumatic brain injury.

While Vivian waited inside the medical tent, a Casualty Assistance Officer (CAO) from Brigade notified her father.

"Sir, your daughter, Captain Chiu, has been injured in an attack. She is okay, Sir. She's been evacuated from the field. She's safe, and being evaluated and treated for minor injuries," the officer said.

"Can I talk to her?"

"Not at the moment, Sir, but I assure you she is safe."

Vivian didn't get to speak to her father.

Jon stayed for as long as he could, just three days. The time didn't matter to Vivian. He'd come. He was with her, and as long as he was, Vivian felt safe. No harm would come to her. She'd be lost without him—they'd be lost without each other.

For those three days, they exchanged the roulette wheel of a soldier's life, took their chips off the table and walked away with their winnings—each other. The gamble would start again, the respite temporary, but for now they had each other. And that's what Vivian needed. Jon, too.

Not long after Jon's return to Kandahar, Vivian and the other soldiers involved in the Taliban's botched attempt to kill them boarded a medevac Black Hawk to Kandahar. Medical ordered more evaluations. The CSH at Kandahar boasted an MRI. Every member of the team had blast-related trauma. Healing from moderate TBI takes time, rest, fluids, some pain meds for headache, not much more, that's de rigueur for that injury.

In the weeks that followed, Vivian began to struggle. She squinted against even the softest light, struggled to turn her head to the left or right without becoming dizzy. At her desk, simple math and basic reports confused her. Her speech had become thick and lazy. Even the slightest physical activity left her easily fatigued. During the night, sleep became elusive.

She needed more recovery time.

For ten days in Hawaii with Jon, Vivian, the former girl ballerina turned woman soldier, rested, slept, dreamed. The girl in her dreams loved to stretch, to pose, to point her toes, to swirl and twirl and leap! She had practiced every day. Long before she understood complicated footwork or slid her feet into ballet slippers, she learned how to coordinate her arms and legs and engage her entire body.

As she grew, Vivian slipped from the childhood dancer into adolescence. Her changing body rebelled against the demands of ballet. In high school, with encouragement from her father, she joined Junior ROTC. The young woman she was becoming gained muscle from the military training. Vivian left the ballet barre.

Her father watched.

Kung-Ming Chiu, a proud Chinese immigrant, a single parent since before Vivian's first birthday, encouraged his daughter to serve the country. He taught her to remember where her family had come from. The third of seven children, an outcast in his homeland, Kung-Ming had escaped communist China with his father and brothers, Vivian's uncles, when he was just a boy. A government official with anti-communist sentiments, Kung-Ming's father feared for his family and his own life. He gathered his wife and sons and fled, becoming one more family among the thousands of Nationalist soldiers and government officials crossing into Hong Kong in the mid-1950s. They became fugitives, living day-to-day in Rennie's Mill, a former industrial complex turned refugee camp. By the early '60s Kung-Ming, his father, grandfather, and brothers made their way to the United States, political refugees, guests of a young president named John F. Kennedy, the man who signed the Migration and Refugee Assistance Act into law.

Kung-Ming loved his adoptive country. Time and circumstance prevented him from serving in the military, but his desire to fight for America burned deep inside of him. He devoured books, movies, and television shows depicting the American military. Father and daughter time, an indecorous weekly television routine, became its own tour of duty through shows like *Tour of Duty*, *Combat!*, *China Beach*, even *M*A*S*H*.

Vivian stayed enrolled in ROTC. Some subtle and more overt influences began to insinuate themselves. In her early years of high school, ROTC cadet Vivian Chiu attended a leadership seminar at Camp Pendleton. She passed through the gate, guarded by Marines without interruption since 1942. During the Vietnam War, Marines, tens of thousands of them, young men, boys mostly, passed through the same gate on their way to Vietnam.

One of the speakers, a young Vietnamese student, a boy who'd taken the American name Andy, spoke eloquently about how the United States welcomed his family after they fled Vietnam. The irony may have been lost on Vivian, but not Andy's message. She took note. The experience prompted her to look at her own family. Her father, given a chance at freedom, had made a life here in the United States after fleeing communist China.

Andy's story changed the course of Vivian's life. In that moment, the idea of serving the country took hold of her. Like a seed in fertile ground, her desire grew and blossomed, leading her to the fields of West Point where she met Vietnamese-American plebe underclassman Jon Cochran, her future husband. In 1970, while serving in Saigon, Jon's father met and married Jon's mother.

———————

In Hawaii, Vivian and Jon stayed in each other's arms, anchored in the depth of their love for each other. The days passed. Vivian exhaled. Comforted by the closeness of her husband and distance from the war, Vivian gradually regained her balance. She didn't talk about the Wesh-Chaman attack. The words for what she witnessed left her. She put the immediate sorrow at the death of the boy and the wounds of her fellow soldiers behind her, making room once again for the good things in her life. *At least—for now.*

The worry-free days in the sun, hours of uninterrupted sleep, seemed endless; but the return to Afghanistan, forestalled for as long as the Army would allow, had reached its "best if used by" date. Vivian and Jon returned to Spin Boldak and Kandahar.

Vivian went to work poring over reports, wading through a stack of paperwork piled on her desk. Amid the paperwork she found a Purple Heart certificate, an order that would later become part of her permanent military records. She read the citation, looked at the certificate, took a deep breath, and stared at the wall. The feeling that the award might be more honor than she had earned gnawed at her. She decided to refuse the medal. Others had been injured far worse in the attack. Other soldiers before her had lost limbs, bore the scars of wounds from small-arms fire or shrapnel, burns from WP. Surely, they deserved the award more than she did.

The Army insisted. The battalion executive officer (XO) recognized that some individuals might seek more visibility and acknowledgement than they deserve, but in Vivian's case, as well as the entire team, their injuries were real. Soldiers, warriors, none of them had sought out the award.

At the end of the day, the XO, adamant that Vivian accept the award, had been right. Cuts and nicks from shrapnel, insignificant, had gone unnoticed, but Vivian had sustained TBI from the blast. She'd been lucky—and wounded. The XO pressed. Vivian accepted the award. She earned it.

Days later, Vivian and Jon found an unexpected kindness in the cruel world around them, Jon's unit had been moved from Kandahar to Spin Boldak. Husband and wife, two soldiers in the middle of a war, could now and would now live together. Vivian tacked a placard on the door of what had become their home away from home. Before they stepped over the threshold, hand in hand, Jon smiled at the sign, especially the acronym (*FWD*) written in fine print, an inside joke the couple shared.

Home Sweet Home
Cochran Residence *(FWD)*

In the world outside the wire, violence against American soldiers, and Afghanis sympathetic to Americans, worsened. Vivian and Jon needed six more months to outwit the war. Days turned into weeks. Jon, an infantry captain in charge of a combat platoon, led his soldiers into harm's way, the missions redundant: protect a school for girls, escort a convoy or an intelligence team, display a show of force, or simply go looking for bad guys. Vivian, an intelligence officer riding a desk, ventured outside the wire less frequently.

During interludes between Jon's missions, living together offered a bittersweet respite. At night they sat outside, admiring crimson sunsets, whispering a pledge to each other. Since life outside the wire didn't offer the promise of a return, Vivian and Jon agreed to always say goodbye, never "see you when you get back." In their minds, goodbye was better than a promise to return, a promise neither one could guarantee.

This was the world they lived in, waking together each day to greet the sun, holding hands at night as crimson sunsets disappeared beneath the horizon, and always—always— sharing a few final moments when Jon found Vivian for a final goodbye before a mission. They developed a routine.

Routine became ritual.

Before he'd roll out, Jon would seek Vivian out. Out of view, they'd wrap their arms around each other, the embrace fierce. They'd stand together, saying little or nothing at all, letting the silence wash over them. A kiss and a final parting buffered them against the uncertainty. Infantry soldiers own many nicknames: grunt, ground-pounder, 11A. Jon rolled into trouble so often, soldiers in his platoon dubbed him "Kaboom."

Each time Jon walked away, leaving his shadow behind, Vivian commanded herself to be brave. More than once, she fought back tears. And more than once, she'd watch the platoon roll out, leaving behind a cloud of billowing dust, the roar of the departing Humvees and MRAPs filling her ears.

She waited and wondered, and sometimes while she waited, Vivian could slip into the comms center and listen to radio chatter. Voices, too broken and obscured by hissing static, offered little comfort. On rare occasions live video imaging feeds of Jon's platoon outside the wire offered shadowy images moving in and out of harm's way. More often than not, she stood outside the ops or comm center once Jon's platoon engaged insurgents or Taliban. Milling about outside she'd wait for word from someone inside, accepting that what she could not hear or see was her husband on the ground—outside the wire and engaged with the enemy.

Afghanistan. Early May 2011.

The cruel Afghan winter had passed its torch. By late April into early May, American soldiers stepped up activities outside the wire. Each time Jon was scheduled to roll out, he'd wake at zero dark thirty. Vivian, too. They'd have chow together, then go back to the CHU. Vivian would watch him strap on his battle rattle, sometimes holding out the next piece of gear for him to slip into. They didn't say much. Jon had his own soldier's routine, personally fitting on each piece of gear, an intimacy that he preferred and Vivian respected.

Days blurred together. Sometime during the first week of May, Jon rolled out on a mission to check Taliban activity in a nearby town. "We might get aerial reconnaissance support today, Predator drone," he told Vivian.

"Maybe I can get inside the ops center and watch," Vivian said, shrugging her shoulders.

Later that morning, inside the operations center, Vivian peered over the shoulder of a soldier. She watched real-time video of Jon's platoon. They rolled up to a small village in Humvees and dismounted. Danger hid in many places. Vivian could see the black images of the platoon moving toward other shadowy figures hiding and moving around buildings that Jon led his soldiers toward. She watched, terrified. She could see the bad guys, everyone in the room could.

"They don't know Taliban is there," she whispered, talking more to herself than anyone in the room. "C'mon, somebody has to alert them."

She prayed that the video feed wouldn't blur into a big shadowy mushroom cloud, an explosion that would mean dead Americans. The platoon stopped. Images on the screen froze. Bad guys moved first. The Taliban retreated, slinking off. Shadows in search of each other, faded. *No contact.* The screen calmed, blinked—went blank. By nightfall, Jon returned. The war, jealous of the love that Vivian and Jon shared, trying to undo them, had been thwarted again.

A handful of days slipped by.

Boredom. Routine. A soldier's life.

Living together in a war zone had become an intricate paradox. During the day Vivian and Jon went in different directions. At night, tucked away in their CHU, a "life-sized shoebox," shut off from everything around them, they slept in each other's arms. Even a little time out of harm's way made them feel safe, but the war waited just outside their window. What they could weave together during the night could easily be unwound in the morning light.

Days went by. Jon had a new mission.

Sent to a Taliban hotspot, the village, Lowy Kariz, Jon's

mission was to discourage insurgent activity in the area. Lowy Kariz was bad business. The village's proximity to the Pakistan border had made it a preferred location for insurgents trying to move weapons, IEDs, and contraband from Pakistan through Kandahar.

Taliban had been intimidating the villagers for years. Whenever American soldiers made their presence known, Taliban, hoping to use the location as a staging area for frequent ambushes, would go into hiding. Over the years American forces had suffered high losses in that area. Time had come to shake up the Taliban once again.

Jon woke first, dressed, and left to perform PCCs and PCIs, precombat checks and inspections with his soldiers. Done, satisfied, he met Vivian for morning chow. They ate in silence then walked back to their CHU for a final goodbye. No matter how many times she'd been through it, Vivian always dreaded the moment.

Hours later, she stood outside the comms center at Jon's unit headquarters, checking with soldiers who knew Jon was her husband.

"Nothing to report yet, Ma'am," a soldier told her.

She waited.

Jon's platoon made contact. Outside, out of hearing, all Vivian could do was wait. The sounds of battle, small-arms fire, shouts, explosions, the clipped, coded dialogues, all she could do was imagine the scene. She walked back to her brigade center and waited. Information had to be routed, first from the battlefield to Jon's company, then to his unit headquarters. The trail of communications eventually led back to brigade, to Vivian.

She waited.

Hours slipped away. Someone from Jon's unit ran into the brigade operations center, shouting, "Ambush! IED! IED!" Vivian's S3 hurried out of the building. She ran after him, stopped him.

"Sir, that's Jon's platoon. What can you tell me?"

He stared at her. "Nothing, Captain. I don't know what's happened yet. There's been an explosion. That's all I've got so far. When I know more, I'll find you myself. Right now, we just don't know."

She waited.

The day disappeared. The FOB grew dark. Hours had passed since anyone had contact or new information. The officer, the S3, found Vivian standing with others outside of brigade operations center. She felt his hand on her shoulder—turned and stared. Tears she'd tried to control spilled down her face.

"Captain, I have news," he said, then lifted his hand from her shoulder. "Your husband is okay, so are his men."

Vivian felt her knees buckle. She fought the overwhelming wave of emotions that washed over her. Keeping a grip on her composure, she saluted the S3 and returned to her CHU to wait for Jon's return. All day she'd felt death close by, hovering. The war had come closer than any day Vivian could remember. It moved on, but not before leaving its footprint on her heart. Not all scars are visible, sometimes you have to look inside.

She'd watch her warrior husband roll out again, and again, *and again,* for the remainder of their tour together. And sometimes, sometimes, Jon would watch her do the same. Each time, they'd say goodbye and wait for the other to return. Each time they'd hold their breath until they could once again hold each other.

They hadn't been much more than teenagers when they met as cadets at West Point, two first generation Asian Americans, a young Chinese American woman and an even younger Vietnamese American man.

Together they serve.

Maggie

DESTINED FOR MORE

"Bagram, oh that's like a stateside base, just in a foreign country. It's safe."

—*Anonymous Soldier*

FROM HER HOSPITAL bed at Walter Reed, Bethesda, the President's hospital, Specialist Maggie Bilyeu heard the *thump, thump, thump,* of several helicopters. Earlier that morning, Secret Service bomb-sniffing dogs padded through halls and into rooms, part of a full security sweep of the building.

For days prior, whispered rumors had drifted through the hospital wards.

Did you hear Obama's coming through?
Michelle is too. Least that's what I heard.

Maggie turned toward the sound. She looked through a window in time to see four green-and-white helicopters, "White Tops," the nickname for the President's helicopters. One of the helicopters carried Barack Obama and Michelle.

Maggie's room filled with somber looking Secret Service

agents, a few hospital officials, and one or two high-ranking members of the military. *Hmm, all this for me?* Before she answered her own question, President Obama walked into the room.

"Mr. President, this is Specialist Maggie Bilyeu," someone important looking said, then turned to Maggie. "Soldier, the President would like to meet with you for a few minutes."

"You asking if it's okay, because he is the President. I mean it's not like he needs permission."

"No Specialist, but—"

The President leaned in. "I've got it from here," he said. "Hello Specialist. I understand we are both from Illinois."

"Well Sir, I'm from Illinois. I was raised on a farm, but you, you're from Chicago. That's not Illinois, that's a whole different place."

The President laughed. "So, so—you mean if I'm from Chicago we're not both from Illinois?"

"That's right, Mr. President. Chicago's not Illinois. Heck, Chicago even has its own flag," Maggie said, then looked around the room.

"You looking for someone?" the President asked.

"Well, Sir, I guess I am. I'm looking for Michelle. I wanted to meet her. No offense, Mr. President, but I thought I'd be meeting her. I was pretty excited when they said Michelle was visiting the hospital."

"So, so, you don't want to meet me?" the President said, feigning surprise, his words halting.

"Oh no, that's okay. You're fine. I was just expecting to meet Michelle. To tell the truth, I really did want to meet her."

"Well, I've, I've got something for you," Obama said, then reached behind him. Someone handed him a Purple Heart medal. He reached down and pinned it to Maggie's hospital gown, then embraced her. She slid her arms around him, surprised that she could easily circle his thin frame.

"Jesus, man, you're all suit. I mean there's nothing to you. You're skinny."

The President released his grip, laughed, backed up a bit, thrust his hand forward. Maggie gripped it and squeezed.

"Oh man, sorry," she said. "That was sort of too hard, didn't mean to hurt your hand."

Barack Obama, the 44th president of the United States, straightened his more than six-foot, unusually thin body, stepped back, shook his head, then grinned at Maggie.

"Specialist," he said, "you get well."

On Bagram, there was no shortage of Afghan or Taliban sympathizers who hated Americans. Halim was one of them, a patient man, polite and unassuming. He'd asked the Americans if he could work for them. Then, after he'd been screened and vetted, he waited. On the day he received a "Red Badge," a clip-on pass that gave him access to Bagram, he joined the thousands of local nationals (LNs) streaming onto the base every day. He worked quietly, employed by a subcontractor, an American engineering and construction firm providing maintenance and construction services on the base.

Within weeks of gaining access to the base, he began to carry out his plan. He slowly, carefully, collected bits of broken glass, pieces of metal, screws, nails—the most coveted prizes. He spoke softly, asked questions about America, feigning interest in the land of his enemy. Over months, the soldiers dropped their guards.

It's Halim, he's okay.

If security assigned to Halim had watched him more closely, they might have noticed that he collected things. Other things that he needed, things that he could not find or steal, he smuggled onto the base.

When Halim left the base, his shift done, he would smile, and surrender his badge. The badge stayed at the gate so it couldn't be stolen or copied. His shifts started early, before dawn. Each morning, in the dark, he'd arrive at the gate carrying his breakfast, flatbread, maybe some lamb or chicken, a boiled egg, and tea, always tea, sweetened with plenty of sugar. No one rummaged through the food he carried.

Inside the maintenance shop, he found a safe place to secret the things he collected. Each time he added something, he'd inspect his collection. *Soon. I'll have enough soon. Soon.*

No one noticed the day he left the base without the vest he'd worn earlier that morning. No one looked that closely. Halim had counted on it. Weeks later he left another vest, one to sew to the other. He laid out the vests, filled them with his lethal collection and an explosive he'd secreted past guards. Finally, he sewed the vests together. He held his handiwork out in front of him, tried it on. The weight felt reassuring.

On Veterans Day, November 11th, 2016, he ate cake with American soldiers. Tomorrow they'd become his target. Notices for an early morning run on the 12th, a final Veteran's Day celebration, had been posted conspicuously for weeks.

———

Specialist Maggie Bilyeu and fifteen other soldiers turned away from a large utility building they called the Clamshell, a metal-framed, fabric building where they had trained for the past six weeks. They'd completed an intensive hand-to-hand-combat training course—optional. They'd been anticipating the final class, the promise of a more untethered practice, a test to see if what they'd learned really worked. But the Clamshell, normally empty at 0500, teemed with soldiers gathered for a post-Veterans-Day run.

"Hey, I didn't know the Shell would be occupied," the

instructor said. "It's not supposed to be. We'll have to about face and see if we can find another building that's open. There's a small gym back at the unit compound. Maybe we can get in there. Let's go." Ready for the workout, all Maggie wore was a T-shirt and sweats. That's all any of them wore.

Halim left the maintenance shop. Unsupervised, he hurried toward his target, the gathering of soldiers at the Clamshell. *Wait. What's this?* Maggie and the group of soldiers, unworried, loud, and unsuspecting, approached. A few of them lit their way with flashlights. Their mental alert systems were switched off. Why not? Bagram's safe.

Halim abandoned his plan. This was good fortune, a vulnerable target close by. He wouldn't have to risk getting caught alone outside. The sky would brighten soon. Now. He'd need to act now, in the half dark, while it would be hard for anyone to see him. He didn't hesitate. His hatred of Americans spurred him on. He didn't shout. Maybe he whispered some final prayer before he turned himself into a weapon, hoping that the suicide vest, his makeshift bomb, pieced together over many weeks, would work. The Americans neared his hiding place. He stepped in front of the soldiers.

Maggie barely saw him emerge from the shadow.

This guy is alone. That's not right. This is going to— But that was all the time she had to think about what might happen. Halim could not to be stopped. Not many suicide bombers could. Unseen, attacking the most vulnerable targets, suicide bombers were willing to die, but in dying they would bring death to their enemies.

Halim was a suicide bomber. Maggie was a target. She took one more step.

The blast blew Maggie's foot out from under her, spun her around, knocked her to the ground. Maggie had been near the front of the group. The bomb ripped her open, leaving a gaping wound, spilling her insides out.

I'm down. Okay, okay. I got hit, that's for sure. Think. Stay down. A minute. I need a minute. Shouts. Jesus, everyone is shouting. Okay, I'm going to get up, look for cover. That's the training, right? Find cover? I'm up. Why isn't anyone else moving? Let me just get off the—Hey, no one is following me. I gotta get back. Man, there's blood everywhere. Oh boy, I think it's mine. It is. I'm falling. Dammit, right on my face. Roll over. Roll over. Holy crap, are those my insides? My foot's on backward. How the hell is my foot pointing behind me?

Oh man, I'm hurt real bad. I'm too far away from the others. Dammit, it's still too dark. Hey. Hey! I'm over here. I don't believe it, no one can see me. Hey! Hey, I know you, don't walk by. That's it. You're limping. You hurt? You see me, right? C'mon you gotta see me. Get closer, that's it, that's it. Ha, I got you, I got your pant leg. That's it. Look down. Yes. Yes. It's me.

You see me. Look. Jesus, my insides are on my lap. Well, that can't be right. Let me, I think I can. . . I'm going to push them back inside of me. Oh, Jesus, this is not good. Don't go. Where are you going? C'mon, don't leave me here.

You're back. Is that a medic with you? A medic, yeah, that's good. Hey, I know you too. Well don't just stand there crying, do something. You're a medic. Yo, quit crying. C'mon, I need you to do something, I mean a tourniquet, stop the bleeding, something, anything, get me on a stretcher. Quit staring . . .

Seven-year-old Maggie Mae listened to her great aunt Linda, who everyone called Diane. "You're going to live here on the farm with me for a while. You'll have your own bedroom."

Maggie's biker dad, a part time father, flitted in and out her life. When her mother wasn't angry with him, she swung her leg over the back of his Harley, wrapped her arms around him, and rode off. Happy until she wasn't, she slipped in and out of Maggie's life. For the next twelve years, Maggie stayed on the farm.

A horse farm's a fun place. There are horse people.

Maggie's aunt was one of them. And, what could be better for a young girl from a broken family than to grow up on a farm around horses? Maggie's aunt didn't waste time. A horse lover who showed horses, she had Maggie Mae walking horses, grooming them, and sitting in the saddle on the back of a pony within weeks of living on the farm.

By the time Maggie turned nine, she rode solo on her own horse, a gift from her aunt. But the gift was more than a horse. Her aunt gave Maggie something to love and care about. As Maggie grew, the young teenage girl she'd become fell in love with horses. Maggie, not the most academically minded, needed something more, something else to work toward, something that she would genuinely care about. Her aunt taught her about horse shows.

Training a show horse demanded hard work. Horse and rider are judged on so many things, things like how to walk, trot, and canter in the ring. To the uninitiated these things might seem routine, but they required discipline and trust. So much of the performance is evaluated on the relationship between horse and rider, the horse's responsiveness to the rider and willingness to work for that rider. Maggie didn't resent hard work and she loved horses.

Some events, like apple dunking, were more fun than discipline. Half race, half apple bobbing, riders lined up at one end of the ring, galloped to the other, jumped from their mount, submerged their heads into a galvanized tub filled with water and floating apples, then bit on to an apple. This was long before anyone had heard of something called COVID. No one seemed to object to the "yuck" factor of having several mouths and noses dunked into the same tub of water.

Maggie excelled at the apple-dunking race. She'd fly down the ring, begin a dismount yards before she'd reach the tub, fling the reins of her horse to boys lined up to catch and hold the mounts, plunge her head into the tub, secure an apple between her teeth, and race back to the finish line. Fearless to the point of recklessness, Maggie intimidated the competition. Other riders rarely stood a chance.

She loved the farm and horses. She loved mischief, too. Maggie made a lot of like-minded friends, mostly boys her age as interested in making mischief as she had become. Levi, a high school classmate, had learned how to weld. The day they decided to build something, birds lined fence rails, and crowded together in trees. Bees and butterflies flitted through a crop of wildflowers. Being outside after a day in the classroom felt right, like a day made just for mischief.

"Let's make a cannon," Levi said.

"Okay, but how?" Maggie answered.

"I've been learning how to weld in shop. Last time we were in the barn I saw some old pipe. I can weld a plate to one end, drill a hole for a fuse. I can get fuse and black powder, get back early enough to try it out. You in?"

"Sure," Maggie said. "What will we use for cannon balls?"

"That's your job. Find some rocks, wrap 'em in aluminum foil, not too big. Round if you can find them. They gotta fit."

They built the cannon, almost a replica of a mortar tube.

"How far do you think it will shoot?"

"Hell, I don't know. I just hope it works."

"Well don't point it at anything, just in case it does."

"You light the fuse."

"Me?"

"Sure, you run faster than me."

Maggie lit the fuse, ran, then turned in time to see it fizzle. She tried again. Again, the fuse fizzled. Determined, she wet her finger, rubbed the spittle on to the pipe, then ran a line of black powder from the pipe, a yard or two behind the cannon. She lit the powder. It blazed a trail faster than she'd anticipated. She learned more about how fast she could run.

Birds roosting on branches just minutes earlier, scattered in alarm. Whirling and twisting into the sky in one spectacular swarm, they cawed and screamed at Maggie and Levi. Horses whinnied. Chickens clucked wildly.

"Son of a bitch, it worked. Let's do it again," Levi said.

"Where'd the rock land?"

"I don't know. I didn't see it."

They spent the rest of the afternoon firing the cannon until it blew apart.

As early as high school, Maggie had thoughts of joining the military. Small town Owaneco, a village no bigger than a minute, population almost 300 if you counted the animals, is a place rich in patriotism. Ask any one of the villagers why, and they'll reply, "We're country bred, corn fed, and proud to be Americans."

Family members before Maggie, even her father, had served in the Marine Corps or Army. They'd fought in World War II and Vietnam. In 1983 her father had been part of the invasion/rescue mission in Grenada.

But Maggie had another passion. She loved animals, especially horses and large animals. By the time she turned nineteen, she enrolled in a nearby community college. The plan: get the general studies requirements out of the way, get good grades, and then apply for pre-med veterinary school. The plan almost worked. The grades were there. The money wasn't. Pre-med veterinary schools, schools like Stanford University, University of Cincinnati, North Carolina State, and others, cost tens of thousands of dollars.

She turned to the military. "Two four-year enlistments," the Army recruiter said. "That will get college paid for. And, besides, if you really want to enlist as an 89 Delta, an Explosive Ordnance Disposal specialist, it requires a four-year hitch."

"I'm in," Maggie said, and signed her first four-year

contract. In October of 2015, a woman eligible to serve in a combat role could join Special Forces. EODs, 89 Deltas, are part of Special Forces.

After boot camp at Fort Jackson, South Carolina, it was on to Fort Lee, Virginia, and 89 Delta school. Farm life and boot camp had toughened Maggie up. Still, at just five-foot-five inches, and just a little over 100 pounds, the physical requirement for EOD looked daunting.

The bomb-suit test is considered one of the most grueling physical assessments in the military. The test, the first step in qualifying for EOD, is pass/fail. And failing means washing out of EOD. It takes months of strength conditioning to be able to move around in one of those things. Maggie had a lifetime of farm work and months of Army boot camp behind her.

The heavy suit weighs 90 pounds, almost as much as Maggie. It's big and bulky, and difficult to maneuver in. If Maggie fell, she probably wouldn't be able to get up. Game over.

"Oh," said the instructor, "did I tell you? You can't disarm a bomb with gloves on. The suit doesn't have gloves. If the bomb blows up, you'll probably survive, but you won't be playing piano. Who wants to go first?"

Maggie stepped forward.

"Okay, Private Bilyeu, suit up."

Even the smallest suit, a man's small, left enough room for almost two of her. The inside of the suit, even in cooler temperatures, turned into a dimension somewhere between a steam room and a sauna. By the time Maggie had finished boot camp and reported for the Advanced Individual Training school, the weather had turned warm.

Unseasonably warm. The fans inside the suit had quit working months earlier.

Maggie began the course. She walked inside a building, then up a flight of stairs, opened a door, then turned to walk back down. But her own sweat and body heat had clouded the face mask. Unable to wipe it away, Maggie violently shook her head from side to side, splashing sweat from her face onto the face mask. She peered through the narrow rivulets streaming down the mask. Back outside she began a walk/shuffle around a short track, probably a quarter-mile runner's course. Before she began, instructors ordered her to stretch out her arms. When she'd fully extended them, an instructor placed a heavy 155-millimeter round across her arms.

"Go for it, Private," he shouted.

Walking in the heavy, ill-fitting suit felt like trying to move through two feet of slime at the bottom of a four-foot mud pond.

"Drop to the ground, Private. Don't drop that shell!" someone shouted.

Maggie knelt, put the 155 on the ground, and went prone.

"Up! Up, Private, up!"

She rose to her knees, then to a genuflecting position, gathered up the shell, then pushed herself to a standing position. Her thighs burned with the effort. Her lungs begged for air. She shuffled forward. She remembered what someone had said about the track, the slower you go, the longer it takes, the more times they'll make you drop. She hurried, trying to get as far around the track as she could before instructors yelled out the command to drop again.

Back at the building, behind it, she staggered into a large sand pit. She knelt, laid the shell in the sand and waited. Instructors began yelling questions at her. The answers were on golf balls buried in the sand. She clawed at the dirt, found a golf ball, not the right one, dug out another, and another, found the right answer. Did it again, then once more.

Back inside the building, she climbed the stairs again, opened the door at the top, shuffled her way into the room, then stood at attention.

"At ease, Private. Congratulations."

Other soldiers helped her out of the suit. There'd been a reason Maggie had gone first. She'd been tipped off that the suits would be passed from soldier to soldier and warned by a friend that putting on a suit someone had already worn would almost make you pass out just from the stench. She'd been quick to take the lead. She watched another soldier don the gear she'd just shed. When he pulled the hood over his head, Maggie's sweat covered his face.

The next day, Maggie failed to pass the first written test of the course. In EOD, there are no second chances; the thought was, if you screw up in the field, you get blown up, maybe blow up a whole bunch of other soldiers with you. Maggie was reassigned—42 Alpha, Human Resources Specialist.

She arrived at Bagram in September of 2016. In a year she could reapply to EOD. For a physical farm girl, riding a desk was about as far away from what she loved doing as she could get. Maggie craved physical activity. When someone suggested taking the self-defense course, she'd been eager to join the class.

The sky shrugged off its cloak. Morning light revealed the carnage. Bodies littered the ground.

"Do something," Maggie shouted at the medic, "do something."

The sight of Maggie, her pleadings, the wreckage that had become her body, shook the medic out of the paralysis that had seized her. She called to others. Another medic moved in. Dozens of soldiers, rifles at the ready, suddenly appeared, forming a perimeter. More medics arrived, more soldiers with stretchers, too. Ambulances rolled up. Soldiers shelved the wounded inside. The ambulances rushed away, sirens blaring.

And still, Maggie lay on the ground. Soldiers moved toward her with a stretcher. Medics helped load her on.

Someone twisted her leg forward with a sickening snap. Her foot pointed toward the sky. She felt hands pulling at her. Medics began cutting away her shredded clothing.

"Stop. Jesus, stop. I'm a gay lady and you guys are trying to look at me naked. Stop," Maggie said, slapping away helping hands trying to save her life. "Get off me. Stop!"

"Knock it off soldier. You're bleeding out, and you're worried about being naked? Let me do my job. I'm trying to save your life. There are no more ambulances, I'm waiting on a truck. Ah, there it is, just slide you onto this backboard . . . strap you . . . on . . . get you to the CSH. Here we go. Up. Not much room. It's a mail truck. Have to leave the doors open. Here we go."

The driver, overreacting, tried to pull away as fast as he could. The mail truck lurched forward with a jolt. Maggie, strapped to the backboard, slid through the open doors. A big Afghan soldier grabbed her in time. They raced to the Combat Support Hospital (CSH), the backboard now a seesaw teetering on the back edge of the truck, the strong soldier desperately hanging on while the scene behind them faded from view.

The shouting had stopped. The cool morning air grew hot and sour. Blood stained the ground. The cacophonous shouts of soldiers, *Take cover! Ambush right! Return fire!* gave way to shock and silence. The cries and pleading of the wounded, *Oh God. Oh God! Help me. Help me! Medic!* were carried off with the dead and wounded, leaving behind a fetid air of silence.

Inside the CSH, chaos reigned. No one had expected a mass casualty attack. The CSH was too small to handle the dozens of wounded being carried in. Medics looked stunned. Doctors shouted orders. The flurry of movement blurred the room.

"Triage, goddammit, triage," a doctor shouted.

Maggie, angry at being naked, shouted orders at everyone. She looked around at others. Less wounded, a few of the men still had clothes on. "This is crazy," she shouted. "Why am I the only naked person?"

"Quiet down soldier," the doctor ordered. "How the hell do you expect us to see what's wrong? Look, look to your left. See that soldier, she's a woman just like you, hurt bad and bleeding out. We cut away her clothes too. We've got to cut away what's left of your clothes to see what the hell is wrong. How do you feel?"

"Nothing seems to hurt."

"That's good, soldier. That's good."

Maggie looked at the other soldier. Her arm, almost severed by the blast, was strapped to her body, barely attached. Soldiers talk their nonsense, their hilarity. Maggie was one of the best at busting on others.

"Hey, I know you," Maggie said. "How's it hanging? Get it?"

The soldier did her best to turn away.

Maggie's adrenaline waned, replaced by pain and resignation. Her face, mottled with splatter of her own blood, looked freckled. *I'm hurt real bad. Tired too. Hell, I guess I'm in the best place I can be. If they can't save me then I'll probably just die. I'm okay with it. Just is what it is . . . I . . . guess . . .*

Days later her eyes fluttered open. The room slowly came into focus. Faces began to look familiar; Aunt Linda, mom, her brother and his wife, even her dad, surrounded her.

"What are they doing in Afghanistan?" Maggie said to no one in particular. "Why would the Army fly my entire family to Afghanistan? It's dangerous here. They should know better."

"Maggie, you're in the States," a nurse said.

"I am?"

"Yes. You were wounded. Do you remember?"

"Yeah, I do now, but how did I get here?"

"You were evacuated to Landstuhl. Doctors slipped you into an induced coma. You're hurt pretty bad. Once you were stable enough to fly, you were transferred here to Walter Reed, Bethesda. Do you recognize everyone?"

Maggie put names to all the faces hovering over her. Mom, dad, her brother and his wife, her aunt too. They needed to see Maggie, but nothing had prepared them for the walk through the corridors of Walter Reed to the ICU where Maggie lay unconscious.

When Maggie did wake up, her sister-in-law tried hard to keep herself together. She fought back tears, tried to remember that she'd been told to stay strong for Maggie. Trying so hard to keep it together, she lost it anyway. The tears came when she saw the tubes and IVs, cuts and bruises, monitors beeping. Maggie looked so helpless. In the end it didn't matter how emotional anyone in the room became. Maggie, slipping in and out of consciousness for the next several days, barely recognized a frown from a smile.

She'd been through several emergency life-saving surgeries. She'd need dozens more to put her broken body back together. She lost part of her stomach, reproductive organs, left breast, and hearing. Traumatic brain injury, the gift that keeps on giving, would leave her with memory loss and balance issues. Surgeons fought to save her leg, but her own orthopedic surgeon later admitted that had she been a man, they would have amputated the leg in the early days of her recovery at Walter Reed, Bethesda.

Three months later, having fought the fight of her life, having endured as many as three and four surgeries a week, Maggie left the ICU. She transferred to the Warrior Transition Unit at Fort Hood, Texas, where she found herself in another battle—a well-intentioned Army surgeon's focus on saving her leg.

Almost three years later, sitting with yet another surgeon, Maggie waited. The surgeon steepled his fingers, poked them beneath his chin, looked off into space, and covered his mouth with his hand. He stroked the side of his chin with a hooked index finger and audibly sighed. He continued to hem and haw. His brow furrowed deeper than a freshly tilled row back on the farm in Owaneco. While he deliberated, Maggie remembered what she'd been told years ago at Walter Reed. "If you were a man, we would have taken the leg."

What the hell is the deal with that? Would I be any less a woman without a leg than a man might be a man if he lost a leg? Did I go through all these surgeries and useless physical therapy because of some belief that women missing a limb are any different than a man with a missing limb? My leg died when I got blown up and someone got me on a stretcher, grabbed my foot and snapped my leg around, snapped it like a twig.

So now, years later, a surgeon looked over x-rays, examined Maggie again and said, "Let's try—"

Maggie stopped him short. "I'm done trying," she said. "The leg is dead. The nerves are gone. I've had enough surgeries on that leg, more than twenty that I can remember. I can't feel anything in that foot. I've broken the foot and didn't know it. If I get cut or scratched and don't know it, an infection could kill me. Trying to learn to walk with a dead leg is wearing out the rest of my body. No more physical therapy. No more braces. No more 'let's try this or let's try that.' I'll have one more surgery on that leg. Take it off."

Mia, Maggie's wife, stepped in, explaining that there wouldn't be any more discussion. They'd made the decision; the leg was coming off.

After surgery, Maggie kept her leg. Keeping an amputated limb is a practice that's generally prohibited. Maggie, along with her wife Mia, decided to keep Maggie's amputated leg.

"We'll keep that leg," they told the surgeon, their voices in perfect unison.

"That's not allowed," a hospital administrator said, "unless, well—there are certain religious exemptions. For example, if you are Jewish, you might qualify for an exemption."

Maggie and Mia looked at each other. Without hesitation, they replied, "Yes." When the hospital presented the leg to Maggie, they asked if she'd like to pray, maybe in Jewish? Maggie bowed her head. Mia, who had learned a Hannukah prayer, recited:

"Al hanisim v'al hapurkan v'al hag'vurot v'al hatshu'ot v'al hamilkhamot she'asita l'avoteinu bayamim hahem bazman hazeh."

"[We thank You] for the miracles, and for the rescue, and for the mighty acts, and for the salvations, and for the wars that You did for our fathers in those days, at this time."

After bringing the leg home, they stored it in a freezer in their basement. Deciding what to do with the leg was more difficult than convincing the hospital to let them keep the leg. They weren't in any rush. The leg wouldn't spoil, and they weren't worried about freezer burn. Before long, Maggie and Mia came up with an idea. Maggie contacted one of the cast members of *Forged in Fire*, Tobin Nieto, a bladesmith capable of crafting hunting knives.

"I want to make a knife with the handle made out of the bone of my amputated leg. Can you help me do that?"

"It will be a first for me, that's for sure, but I've made bone handles out of animal bone and antler. I guess it wouldn't be any different than that. Leg bone is best. It's the easiest to hollow out. If you want it to be recognizable to most people as being an actual bone, you'll do better to leave a joint end on it. So, yeah, I can make it for you or guide you through it, maybe a little bit of both?"

On a Wounded-Warrior-sponsored hunting trip, Maggie used her leg bone knife to skin her kill, a wild boar she speared by hand. "After all," she said, jokingly, "a lot of blood, sweat, and tears went into that knife."

The cries of the wounded have quieted. Blood that stained the ground has washed away. The shouts of soldiers, stilled by time, drift in and out of Maggie's memory. She'd come to Bagram as a noncombat soldier. She'd intended to do her time in country, even if it was behind a desk instead of in a protective bomb suit. Later, she'd have the chance to try 89 Delta again. She wanted more, and she had time. For now, she'd keep her bargain with the Army, ride a desk, serve with honor, continue training her body, and become a good soldier.

Bagram was safe. She'd get through her tour with ease, redeploy stateside, retrain and return, this time as a combat soldier. Maybe it was all a dream. It seems like a lifetime ago. But it wasn't a dream. Maggie served a total of thirteen months of active duty. The scars, the injuries, the wheelchair she sits in, the thoughts that she sometimes cannot capture, all these things are proof that in war, nowhere is safe. But a suicide bomber will never define Maggie Mae Bilyeu. She is so much more than that.

She's dedicated to rehabbing. There are more surgeries. She'll recover from those, too. She is a fighter. The big goal is to get well, to be able to use her prosthetic again, get out of the wheelchair, and reclaim the independence of her earlier life. With her wife Mia supporting her, when surgeries are mostly behind her, she'll hunt, fish, go boating and kayaking. She hasn't been back on a horse yet, but nothing is impossible.

Maggie is only thirty-two-years old and destined for so much more.

Tara

EIGHTEEN MINUTES

When I was fifteen, all I wanted was to go off to some other world, a place beyond anybody's reach. A place beyond the flow of time.

—*Haruki Murakami*

AT NIGHT, lying on a mattress in a barracks at Fort Leonard Wood, hands behind her head, Army Private Tara Kathleen Seaman stared into the dark. Outside temperatures dipped below freezing. January cold seeped through walls of the half-century-old cinder block building. In the morning, before sunrise, she'd being doing pushups in the snow. Unable to sleep, she listened to the sounds of a room filled with soldiers, all of them women. Their heavy breathing, coughs, the rustle of blankets, the complaint of a mattress, kept her awake. She asked herself, "Why the hell did I do this?"

Her feelings for the Army, boredom, resentment, the gradual dawning that maybe, just maybe, joining the Army had been a mistake, gnawed at her. But, as the saying goes,

"The Army, it ain't something you can just up and quit." In her early weeks as a raw recruit, she discovered that the main thing wrong with the Army (besides falling out for physical training at zero dark thirty) was being told what to do and when to do it. Army life didn't feel like the independence she craved; Army life was all about rules.

Tara had never been big on rules.

Anyone who knew her would not have seen a soldier in the girl who'd run away from home a half dozen times before starting high school, certainly not Linda and Kenneth Seaman, Tara's mother and father. Whenever Tara felt some imaginary slight, whatever wrong she believed Linda and Kenneth had inflicted upon her, too strict, not enough freedom, you don't understand me, she ran. Each time she ran, she went a little farther and stayed away a little longer. She even landed in a halfway house for runaways. And still, she ran.

Whenever the reality of street life would catch up with her, always cold, hungry, always at risk, she'd find her way home. Linda kept the door open. Whenever Tara returned, Linda tried to keep her there. Counseling rarely worked. Tara just became angry; Linda became more confused, and the result was always the same. Tara returned to the streets.

Baffled by Tara's troubles, Linda continued to try and rescue her daughter. Kenneth, too exhausted by Tara's antics, or maybe too busy building a life as a commercial pilot after flying helicopters in the Alaska National Guard, didn't take the lead. He left Tara and Linda to figure out how life would work for all of them.

Alaska winters don't have much sympathy for runaways. Eventually the balance shifted. Tara simply tired of street life with its harsh realities. She began to spend more time at home and less time on the streets. She managed her way through high school and into University of Alaska Fairbanks, enrolling in a Criminal Justice program.

When Kenneth decided to move the family from Eagle River, a small town outside of Anchorage, to Oregon, Tara went her separate way. She left college, packed up the few things she owned, one of them a boyfriend, and moved to a little town outside of San Francisco. Almost a year later, she called her mother.

"Mom," she said, "I'm never going to marry this guy. Living with him has cured me of that idea. I've got to get out of here. I don't have a car, or any money. I need help."

Linda and Kenneth drove from Oregon to San Francisco, collected their daughter, no questions asked, and brought her home. Within months, a familiar disquiet began to surface, a feeling Tara recognized and couldn't fight. Full circle, she'd landed back under her parents' roof and into a going-nowhere retail job. At twenty-two, no money, staring at an empty future, she searched for an escape.

Military recruiters come across plenty of people like Tara —young, directionless, aiming for something bigger, but not knowing what that something is, feeling worn out before life has really begun, searching for a way past the dead end in front of them. Tara walked by an Army recruiting office on the way to her dead-end job at Nordstrom. She hadn't given the posters plastered in the windows much attention —until now.

The military. A lot of people join the military. I don't want to go in the Army, though. Maybe the Air Force? How tough could the Air Force be? That's it. I'll join the Air Force.

The Air Force was tougher than she thought. Living an easy life at home, she'd put on pounds. The Air Force turned down her enlistment. She stopped into the Army recruiting office; the Army said yes, conditionally. They gave her a goal. She'd have to meet a qualifying weight standard, pass an enlistment physical, and do it by a specific date. There'd never been much in life that motivated her to push herself as hard as she'd need to. Desperate to get out from her parents' house, more motivated than she'd ever been, Tara worked her butt off—literally. She lost forty pounds, passed the physical, and enlisted, doing it in just two months.

In the world she'd lived in before the Army, Tara had never been sure of her footing. She'd never aimed for anything bigger or farther than staying one jump ahead of the bad things that happened on the street. Army life—structure, direction, discipline—all of it began to nudge her toward more than she'd ever been forced to do before. She completed boot camp in the spring of 2000 and began to find her footing. She wasn't in love with the Army, at least not yet, but by the time she'd enrolled in AIT, training to become an MP, a budding courtship slowly blossomed. MP training captured her interest. Tara flourished. She turned away from a life that until now had been blown sideways, squared her shoulders, and leaned into the wind. Tara was becoming a soldier—a good soldier.

Almost two years later, after garrison duty at Fort Bragg, Tara, ready and in queue for an overseas deployment to Korea, watched as the Twin Towers fell. Army units around the world readied to deploy at a moment's notice. Furloughs were cancelled; soldiers on leave reported back to bases everywhere. Permanent Change of Station (PCS) orders were delayed, changed, or scrapped while the world held its breath.

Country Western singers quickly penned patriotic tunes. Toby Keith promised to "put a boot in your ass." Hank Williams, Jr, growled, "America can survive, America is gonna survive." Alan Jackson, more reflective, asked, "Where were you when the world stopped turning, that September day?" By December, most of the world exhaled. Tara celebrated an uneventful Christmas as part of the 249th MP unit at Camp Humphreys in South Korea.

Although the fighting stopped when North Korea, China, and the United States reached an armistice in 1953, the Korean War, the hot war, had not ended. South Korea did not agree to the armistice. The 249th, the MP unit Tara had been assigned to, part of the US Peacekeeping force in Korea, had a much bigger role than simple garrison duty. Only sixty miles from the DMZ, MP units often were tasked with visiting villages along the DMZ, monitoring and observing activities of locals. MPs accompanied Army infantry and pulled security details for visiting US politicians wanting to steal a look into North Korea. They chased villagers out of decades-old pillboxes and concrete bunkers, usually with a gift, cash, or supplies—and, oh yeah, MPs controlled American tourists looking for souvenirs, especially signs like "Danger! Mine Field."

Tara went out to the DMZ just once. There was much more in store for her at Camp Humphreys. Her platoon sergeant, a chiseled, in shape, spit-and-polish, "High Speed" sergeant major, took a personal interest in Tara. He worked with her, getting her in the best physical condition of her life, and teaching her how to soldier at an even higher level than she'd already reached. She modeled his approach to soldiering.

She sought out more responsibilities. After going through a confusing first few weeks in Korea, she realized the need for a more formal orientation program. Using her own experiences, Tara developed a dual orientation and training program for US Army personnel and Korean soldiers, KATUSAs, Koreans attached to the US Army. The program became known as the School of Standards.

KATUSAs, Tara quickly learned, took orders by consensus. Tara would give an order; the Korean soldiers stood and stared. One soldier, probably the one who had a basic understanding of English, would turn to the others. They'd circle. An animated conversation, complete with quick hand gestures, nodding, and shaking of heads, generally went on for several minutes. Grunts, oohs, and aahs, would fill the air. Eventually, the spokesman would turn back to Tara.

"Okay, Sergeant, okay," he would say, indicating that he understood. More often than not, something got lost in the translation.

It was funny, until it wasn't. On the rifle range, Tara instructed a young KATUSA to point his rifle downrange, towards targets. He nodded vigorously, shouted the standard Korean reply, "Okay, Sergeant, okay," then executed an unexpected about face, his weapon now pointing at Tara, weapons instructors, and soldiers in queue. Everyone ducked. The Korean flashed a smile. Tara turned him around, muttering an inaudible obscenity.

Almost two years later, after arriving in Korea as a spec 4, Staff Sergeant Tara Stewart (married/divorced/kept the name) redeployed back to Fort Leonard Wood. She attended NCO school, part of the requirement for her rank. Anxious to continue her climb through the ranks, Tara met with her platoon sergeant major for a career assessment.

"I want to become one of the fastest women ever to become a sergeant major—Sergeant Major," she said. "I want to do a tour as a Drill Instructor. I enjoy training new soldiers, showing them the opportunity the Army has shown me."

"Wait on Drill Instructor school, Sergeant. If making rank is your goal, what will help you more is deploying to a combat zone. Become a drill instructor after a tour in Iraq or Afghanistan. The 463rd MP company is slated to deploy to Iraq by the end of the year. Put in for a transfer. I'll see that it gets approved and you can join them."

To train up for the deployment, complete and certify all the "squad lanes," simulated field exercises to declare squad leaders "battle ready," takes months. By the end of 2005, the 463rd was ready. A lot of the training had been grueling; the intent, save the lives of soldiers. The training included weapons training, map reading, land navigation, calling in life saving air support and medevacs, tactical response to ambush or IED attacks, and extensive emergency life-saving first aid.

Tara learned how to insert IVs and keep a soldier from bleeding out on the battlefield.

Almost all missions in Iraq and Afghanistan call for mounted roll outs in up-armored Humvees and MRAPs. Newer, heavily armored, and more powerful, hardtop Humvees were gradually replacing the twenty-year-old rag tops, the soft-canvas-topped Humvee. One of the squad lanes included extensive training on piloting a Humvee. Heavy, they are slow to stop and quick to roll over, despite the vehicle's unusual width. Iraq's weather extremes include a rainy season that creates mud hazards. Even Iraq winters are muddy.

A simulated training exercise called for squad leaders to deliberately have their teams plunge Humvees into a large mud pit. One by one, a team would roll forward and sink the Humvee up to the doors. The Humvees now unable to roll out of the pit under their own power, squad leaders had to direct their team leaders to get the Humvees mobile, and to do it quickly. A disabled vehicle, especially a Humvee full of soldiers, is a coveted target of opportunity for Iraqi insurgents.

SSgt Tara Hutchinson (married again) led her team into the mud pit. Wheels spun. Mud rooster-tailed behind the Humvee, splattering anyone and everything in its path with a hail of mud. Soldiers had to exit any way they could. Boots and uniforms would be a nightmare to clean. Not everyone was happy. Tara took charge, directing her team to drag a winch cable through the mud, find something to attach it to, in this instance a tree, and pull the Humvee free. Soldiers would be cleaning more than boots and uniforms; Humvees would have to be scrubbed clean.

By the time the Humvees had been cleared from the mud pit, soldiers' moods had fouled. Tara took note. She scooped up a large wad of brown, viscous mud and flung it at the nearest soldier. *Game on!* Mud flew everywhere, hitting soldiers with thuds and splats. Exhausted, laughing, and relieved, the soldiers, and their lady squad leader, SSgt Tara Hutchinson, poised for a picture. Soldiers flanked both sides of their squad leader.

Tara, once a troubled kid on the street, had become a respected leader of men.

By Christmas, the 463rd was ready for deployment. Tara's mom visited with her during Christmas week. Just after the New Year, 2006, Tara and her soldiers boarded a C-17 bound for Kuwait, the traditional staging point for troops on the way to Iraq. Almost twenty-four hours later, Tara stepped onto an airfield in Kuwait.

By the middle of January, the 463rd stood waiting to board a C-130 that would fly them into Baghdad. From there they'd roll out to a FOB west of the Green Zone. The day turned into a classic military marathon, "hurry up and wait." Ordered out onto the runway by 0800 on what had to have been an old Kuwait Army airfield, Tara and the 463rd waited late into the night to board the airplane.

They had plenty to look at during the day.

Evidence of Saddam's decades-old botched attempt to annex Kuwait was still visible. A solitary wall near the runway, pockmarked by bullets, served as a stark reminder of the brutality of Iraq's former dictator. Kuwaiti soldiers had been lined up against that wall and executed by Iraqi firing squads.

Forewarned about a rapid descent, an evasive maneuver to avoid any potential enemy fire, Tara still turned white as a sheet when the plane seemed to plunge into a steep dive. She dug her fingernails into her thighs and held her breath.

"Holy crap," she muttered. "That scared the hell out of me."

One of the other NCOs sitting near her looked pale. "Don't even think about puking," Tara said.

The flight crew lowered the rear ramp of the C-130. Soldiers filed out. Tara's eyes adjusted to the dimly lit airfield. She walked side by side with other leaders of the 463rd. Even in the dark their MP arm patches were conspicuous. A Special

Forces soldier, maybe a Navy Seal, hard to tell—he sported a full beard, only Special Forces and Seals grew beards—pushed a woman toward Tara. The woman, hands bound behind her back, a black hood pulled over her head her over her head, stumbled forward. She regained her balance just a few feet in front of Tara.

"Your patch, you're MP, the new unit," the bearded soldier said.

"I am. We all are," Tara replied.

"I need you, a woman. I need you to search this prisoner."

"What?"

"She's a woman. I need another woman to search her."

"Dude we just landed. There's gotta be someone else to take her."

"I need another woman to do this. You're the only woman around. Do it."

"I can't," Tara said, her voice matching the force of the soldier's.

"Aw, Christ, what the hell am I supposed to do with her?"

"There has to be someone that can search her," Tara repeated, while the soldier shuffled the prisoner away from the men and women exiting the C-130.

"That was pretty weird," Tara said, turning to another squad leader standing nearby. "I mean how the hell did he expect us to do anything?"

"Yeah, it was. Welcome to Iraq, I guess."

The 463rd left the Green Zone for a FOB west of Baghdad, FOB Victory. Tara ramped up quickly, taking command of four teams, soldiers, medics, and interpreters that would make up her squad. She relied on her training and experiences in Korea. Parts of her duties in Iraq, training and supervising Iraq police, were similar to training KATUSAs.

Creating a functioning Iraq civilian police force came with challenges. Plenty of men vied for the good paying job. Not all of them had what it takes. Tara and her squad trained the Iraqis in the everyday responsibilities of police work. "I'm going to turn you guys into COPS," she told them. She insisted they wear the standard Iraqi police uniform without personal regalia, taught them how to man a police station, schedule shifts, keep records, question a detainee, perform everyday law enforcement tasks—and maintain weapons discipline. She eliminated the practice of firing a weapon into the sky as a form of celebration.

"Not cool, you guys, not cool, no more of that," she ordered.

She quickly overcame the strong cultural bias against women. The Iraqis trusted her. There were other women on FOB Victory, a few in the 463rd, but none on Tara's squad, a relief to Tara. She always asked more of the few women she'd trained with or outranked. Sure, it was a double standard, but whatever one woman soldier did poorly quickly reflected on all women soldiers. If a man screwed up, well he was just a bad soldier, a screw-up, a one-off. When women soldiers messed up, it was generalized; she's a woman, they're all like that. Not having to hold another woman to a higher standard lessened the burden on Tara.

Aside from a mountain of paperwork, Tara loved her new role, her soldiers, and the task of creating stand-alone, independent Iraqi police facilities. She continued to train up her men, building teams that complemented strengths and weaknesses, keeping them sharp, tactical, alert, and squared away.

"I want a high-speed squad," she said, using her term for competent soldiers. She warmed to the challenge of doing the same thing with the Iraqis. The awkwardness she'd felt during the first few days in Iraq had disappeared. By early February, just a few weeks into her tour, Tara had won the respect of her men, and the Iraqis.

There had been one more piece of business she'd needed to get out of the way, that or get redeployed home. Tara had reached the end of her first enlistment. An Army career, something that had seemed unlikely for the once-runaway teenager, now became her future. Her re-enlistment contract caught up with her during the first few days in Iraq. She signed. With that out of the way, she could fulfill the twelve-month tour.

It didn't last long.

Winter weather in Iraq fluctuates wildly. Sub-tropical aridity of the Arabian Desert clashes with the subtropical humidity of the Persian Gulf, creating extremes. Rain let loose on the 463rd almost every day for the first two weeks of February.

Any road that wasn't blacktop or that had been damaged in the fighting turned to mud, often shin deep. Squads rolled out, mindful of the weather or, more precisely, the mud. The roads leading to and from FOB Victory were a mix, some unpaved, some blacktop, many somewhere in between. Roads in disrepair posed a two-fold threat: Humvees could become bogged down in mud, and piles of rubble lining the sides of the roads provided perfect camouflage for hidden IEDs.

On the morning of February 14th, the rain stopped. Tara's squad had been ordered to roll out, the mission, a police station inspection. By mid-morning, they formed a convoy, four up-armored Humvees, Tara leading from the front—her choice. First stop, convoy out, pick up one of the interpreters. Unlike most of the "terps" that lived on base, this interpreter lived off base with his family.

Trouble started just a few klicks outside the wire, about twenty minutes from the FOB. Coolant spit through heater vents in one of the Humvees. The cab filled with a sickening mist of radiator coolant. The team leader of the Humvee got on his comm.

"We've got to stop," he radioed. "We've got some kind of leak or something. We're getting sprayed with anti-freeze."

"Roger that," Tara said, ordering the convoy to roll to a stop. "Stay in your vehicles. Let me check it out, see if it's anything we can fix quickly, otherwise we'll head back to the FOB. Follow ops orders. Sweep 360, cover the rear, the front, all parameters, everyone, stay sharp."

Tara, in full battle rattle, ran back to the partially disabled Humvee.

"Okay, what's the—never mind, I see it, smell it, the cab is filled with radiator fluid. You guys are drenched. We can't fix this. We're rolling back to base, cover your faces, use your Keffiyeh, don't breathe that stuff in, and use your goggles, keep your eyes protected. You'll be okay, we're only a few klicks out. Everyone except the driver, get in the back. Close the vents, stuff some rags into them. Just hope we don't lose too much coolant and overheat. You good?"

"Roger that, Staff Sergeant."

"Alright, let's move out."

The convoy limped back to FOB Victory. Tara checked in with the platoon sergeant major. She explained the trouble.

"So, you didn't complete the mission?" he asked.

"No, Sergeant Major, I guess we'll secure the other vehicles and roll out again in the morning."

"Negative. Get back to transportation, secure a replacement vehicle, and complete the mission. Get the terp, roll out, and inspect the police station; complete the mission."

With a momentary mutinous, "Aw, Sergeant Major, it's mid-afternoon. Go back out now," she said. "You gotta be kidding. It's already late afternoon."

"It is, so you'd better get moving."

"Roger, Sergeant Major. Happy Valentine's Day."

"What's that, Staff Sergeant?"

"Happy Valentine's Day, Sergeant Major. It's Valentine's Day."

A soldier in the transportation group, a friend of Tara's, looked out for her. He knew the idiosyncrasies of most of the vehicles in the motor pool and tried to outfit Tara and her squad with the better performing Humvees. When the squad delivered the disabled Humvee, he pulled a good truck from a row of mission ready vehicles.

"I like this one, Staff Sergeant. It's one of the newer ones. Bring it back in one piece."

"Roger that, thanks for watching out for my squad," Tara said. "I'll try to bring her back just the way you gave her to me."

"Good luck."

Outfitted with the replacement Humvee, team three, operational again, slipped into queue. The squad rolled out, headed for the original destination. Ten mikes out, the convoy reached an overpass. They rolled through and approached a section of the route known as Race Track Road. The road curved slightly, just enough to create the quickest blind spot. Leading her squad out of the curve, Tara, in country for just a month, knew trouble when she saw it. She spotted rubble on the side of the road, broken up asphalt that had been hidden by the bend in the road—something out of the ordinary, fresh, not weathered by rain and dust. Trouble. Tara knew it. Before she could halt the squad, she heard the explosion. Her eyes reflexively closed against the flash. The Humvee, her Humvee, filled with smoke. Through the haze she could see blood spurting from her driver's neck. She looked at the others, their faces covered with dust and flecked with blood.

I'm in charge. It's my show. These are my men. Check on them. Driver, you okay. Thumbs up. Wait, what? You're bleeding badly, how the hell are you okay? Wow, I feel strange. My leg feels like it's on fire. Should I look? Don't look. You gotta look. Geezus, my leg—is—on—it's on fire. What the hell! Where's my other leg? Oh, man. My leg is all torn up. Is that bone? Yep. Bone. Flesh too. Wow, I'm losing blood, a lot of blood. Hey, how long can I lose that much blood and survive? Get out. I gotta get out. C'mon Tara, open the door. You locked it fool. Slow down. Don't panic.

In shock, her brain functioning in slow motion, Tara understood that unless the bleeding was slowed or stopped, she was going to die. She unlocked the door, but something still held her captive. Her Beretta 9mm, the pistol all MPs carried, had been blown off with her leg, but a lanyard she'd attached to it had wrapped around a radio mount. Tara, tethered to the Humvee, was rapidly bleeding out. Still concerned about her men, she ordered the gunner to evacuate the Humvee.

"I can't, Staff Sergeant, both my legs are broken."

Sergeant Brydges, the assistant squad leader, pulled on the driver's door. Stuck. He pounded on it, then pulled with a newly discovered strength. The door flew open. He pulled the driver out, laid him on the ground. Soldiers rendered first aid. Brydges turned back to Tara, tugging on her.

"Stop! For God's sake, stop! I'm stuck," she shouted.

Brydges knew he had to stop the bleeding. He pulled off his belt, cinched it around what was left of Tara's leg. Pain shot through Tara's body. Her boot and uniform had melted to her other leg. Brydges spotted the lanyard, pulled out his Ka-Bar knife, and sliced the line in two. He grabbed Tara's leg, almost severed, cradling it, trying to keep it from falling away from Tara's body while he pulled her out and carried her to another Humvee, placing her gently inside. A younger soldier jumped behind the wheel, u-turned the Humvee, and raced back to FOB Victory. A medic searched Tara's body, looking for a place to insert an IV. He rubbed alcohol on Tara's neck.

"Don't even think about putting that needle into my neck," she screamed.

"There's no place else—"

"I don't care, don't you dare stick me in the neck, I'll kill you, I swear."

The medic hesitated.

The insurgents did not launch a full-on ambush.

At FOB Victory, Tara was lifted from the Humvee and placed on a stretcher. Conscious, she looked at her leg. Barely attached, the leg flopped over, twisting awkwardly. The sight of a boot heel where her toe should have been jolted Tara out of shock. Fire raced through her body.

Oh my God, this hurts, and my leg, what's up with my leg?

Her eyes fluttered. Her heart stopped.

Doctors started an IV, began manual resuscitation, strapped an oxygen mask to her face loaded her onto a Black-hawk—still no heartbeat. The Blackhawk lifted off, ferrying Tara's lifeless body to the Green Zone. Eighteen minutes to a large CSH and a last chance to save her life.

Inside the CSH, doctors fought to revive her.

"How long, how long has she—"

"Eighteen minutes, maybe more, Doctor, Pupils fixed and dilated. We're losing her—"

"No, we're not. Clear!"

"Nothing, Doctor."

"Again. Clear."

"Doctor—"

"Again."

"Last time, do it. Clear!"

The emergency room fell silent. The doctor hesitated, then beat on Tara's chest.

"C'mon soldier. C'mon. Nobody dies here today. Do you hear me, nobody dies!"

A beep, two, more.

"She's back, Doctor."

"Alright, let's get to work."

With her strong heart beating again, Tara gave doctors the

chance they needed to win the fight for her life—a fight that was just beginning.

Polytrauma. How neat and tidy it sounds. One word to categorize the list of multiple injuries that should have killed Tara. She suffered from burns on her left leg, the one still attached. Heat from the blast (something civilians don't know or think about) melted her boot and parts of her gear, her uniform too, searing everything into her flesh. Internal injuries, the full extent unknown. Blast trauma. Head injury complicated by a loss of blood flow while her heart had stopped beating, multiple cuts, bruises, hematoma, imbedded shrapnel, and a leg, that, if doctors didn't amputate, would have fallen off. Serious infection set in almost immediately.

The miracle that she'd come back from eighteen minutes without a heartbeat of her own was just the beginning. She'd need more medical care than she could get in Iraq if she was going to live. She been ferried from the battle field, back to FOB Victory, helicoptered to the Green Zone, revived, ferried to the joint air base at Balad, flown to Landstuhl, stabilized and flown to Walter Reed in the US, and finally to Brooke Army Medical Center in Texas (BAMC).

Through all of the transfers, emergency care, and immediate life-saving surgeries, Tara flitted in and out of consciousness. On the flight from Landstuhl, Tara opened her eyes.

"Hey there," an Army captain nurse said. "You're still with us."

Unable to speak, Tara looked at the captain.

"Look soldier," the captain said, "you're going to be okay. It's all going to work. You're going to get well. I'm going to sit right here with you until we're back in the States. I'm not going anywhere. Anything you need, just tug on my sleeve.

We'll figure it out, and I'll get it. I'll keep you comfortable. Trust me, soldier, you're going to be okay."

Kenneth Seaman, Tara's father, a commercial airline pilot and former National Guard pilot must have still had friends in the Guard, or former soldiers he'd served with who owed him favors. Once he learned of Tara's injuries, once he understood that his daughter was in serious condition, he pulled strings, scheming his way onto a military transport, a C-17, a flying ICU bound for Landstuhl. As he touched down in Germany, Tara, aboard a smaller, faster jet aircraft, was already airborne.

Kenneth chased his daughter half way around the globe. He hopped a C-17 ferrying wounded soldiers to Walter Reed, missed Tara again, then followed her to BAMC. There he caught up with his daughter. He stood by the bedside, staring at her, his first sight of her in several years. Her swollen cheeks and eyes, puffed up like a pummeled boxer's face, unnerved him. Her breathing was deep, solemn, rhythmic, but she breathed on her own. He listened to the whirring, buzzing, and beeping of equipment that signaled life.

"My God," he whispered. "What have they done to you?"

Throughout the years, his relationship with Tara had strained past a breaking point. Now, seeing her like this, beaten and broken by war, heartbreak overwhelmed him. He choked back a sob. Unable to fight back tears, he cried for his daughter, and the lost years. He noticed a hospital comb on a stand next to Tara's bed. He hesitated, looked at his daughter, tears flowing freely now. He ran a finger over the backbone of the comb, picked it up, and looked at Tara. With the tip of his finger, he slid a strand of hair from her forehead, then slowly, gently he ran the comb through her hair.

Tara's eyes fluttered open. She squinted through the swelling. "Daddy?"

"Yes, it's me. I came as soon as I could."

The softness of his touch, the gentle caress, washed away decades of hurt.

Tara lived off and on, in or around BAMC for the next four years. Multiple surgeries, constant physical and occupational therapies, treatments for infections, dealing with trauma-induced menopause, pain management, regaining as much independence as possible—this was her life.

And it wasn't easy.

Two years after almost losing her life, the struggle to successfully use a prosthetic kept her tethered to a wheel chair. The prosthetic fit well, worked the way it should, and Tara did her best to hold up her end of the bargain with physical thera-pists and prosthetists. She fought through the pain, worked on strengthening her core and all the muscles she need to use to fire up a prosthetic.

None of it worked.

Doctors decided to send her back to Walter Reed. X-rays, MRIs, videos while wearing and walking with the prosthetic, revealed the issue. The adductor muscle, the muscle on the inside on Tara's thigh, was not attached to the femur. The original amputation had left the femur too short to attach muscle to bone. There was no way Tara could pull what remained of her leg forward, movement that she'd need to jolt the prosthetic into motion. No amount of physical therapy, six-pack abs, or the physique of a body builder, would solve the issue. Surgical repair was the only option.

But first doctors would have to add length to the femur. Tara would have to grow her own leg bone.

The initial surgery would demand at least six months of treatment to promote the necessary bone growth. Doctors inserted screws into the femur, a somewhat radical and painful technique that would pull the leg apart, allowing for bone to grow in the gap. The screws needed constant adjustment, generally every three or four days. Doctors instructed Tara in the procedure to turn the screws, just a quarter turn each time. Anxious to recover, impatient to gain her independence, she attempted to speed up the process, and turned the screws aggressively. If a quarter turn was good, a half turn would be better—not. She ruptured the wound; doctors had to operate again. The process started from scratch. This time Tara dutifully adhered to the quarter turn prescribed.

Her good leg needed more surgery, too. The burns to that leg required additional skin grafts to permanently heal. In addition to enduring the painful, tortuous turn of the screws, Tara fought off one infection after another. She stopped counting how many surgeries she'd been going through. She just couldn't keep track. The pain, at times so constant, made her want to quit. The medications to combat infections wreaked havoc on her body. She began to think about giving up. *Maybe, maybe, it's just better to live with this, than go through any more surgeries. I can't stand this anymore, I can't.* Everyone encouraged her. She fought back. Six months later, doctors attached the muscle to the lengthened leg.

Recovery would never be complete. The damage was simply too extensive. Lingering issues remain—Parkinson's Syndrome, the result of the temporary loss of blood to her brain and the blast force trauma. Her body doesn't self-regulate temperature very well. She's been robbed of the chance to have children. Pain is constant.

Her occupational therapist recommended jewelry making, a task that would help her recover fine motor skills. She turned the hobby into a money-making business. She traveled the country, putting on shows, getting orders for her one-of-a-kind pieces. Eventually the hobby, never intended to become a business, became a chore.

2022

Tara might spend a little more time in a wheel chair than she'd like, but she'll have to decide on more surgeries to change that. TBI makes remembering things difficult, and sometimes Tara might say things that may be a little irreverent. She'd be the first to admit that she might shock you with a comment. *Tara, say anything you want!* She lives with her dog, Porkchop; she gardens when she's not traveling. Her mom lives close by. Dad is gone, but Tara will never forget waking up and feeling his touch. "What a gift he left me," she'll tell you. "Even after all the trouble I gave him."

Life is good for the former soldier's soldier, and the girl on the street. What she'd really yearned for early in her life, whether she knew it or not, had been something to care about. She found that in the Army, *leading men.*

Lana

MORE THAN THE BAD THINGS THAT HAPPENED

You can't wait until life isn't hard anymore before you decide to be happy.

— NIGHTBIRDE, SINGER-SONGWRITER

FORMER ARMY SERGEANT Elana Duffy sits comfortably on a large burgundy couch in the living room of her one-bedroom NYC apartment. It's a true one-bedroom, distinct and closed off from the living room and kitchen area, a rarity for this part of the city, Kips Bay, Manhattan. A dozen or more pictures, keepsakes serving as reminders of duty stations and trips, decorate the wall above her.

The collection began innocently enough, a long-ago barter with a street artist; then, as she deployed or traveled, searching local bazaars and markets, striking bargains almost always weighted in her favor became a regular thing. Paintings and drawings from Iraq, Afghanistan, India, Peru, Hawaii, Russia, Prague, more, moved in with her the day she crossed the threshold. There's room for more. Elana still has a lust for travel and adventure.

I've invited myself into her home, her life, and she's

graciously allowed me in. She's comfortable telling her story. I hope I can capture it all. Sometimes, depending on the question, she seems amused. A furrowed brow lets me know she's working at remembering details of decades-old memories. When I ask the wrong question, a nod of the head and a cautionary glance tells me we're not going there.

As she remembers her deployments to Afghanistan and Iraq, puts together the pieces of the puzzle that was her time as a soldier, Elana runs the palm of her right hand over her head, smoothing her dark hair. She lifts her left hand; fingers mingle, pulling the unfettered length into a topknot. Moments later, just as smoothly, she loosens the twist, letting her long hair fall below her shoulders. Her dark eyes shine playfully. The corners of her mouth lift into a subtle grin that turns into a broader, welcoming smile.

She's a young woman. Attractive. Vibrant. To those who don't know her, it would be hard to picture her in combat uniform, full battle rattle, an M-4 rifle hanging across her body.

Annika, one of Elana's cats, makes a cameo appearance. She circles gingerly in Elana's lap. Her long black tail snakes upward, brushing against Elana's cheek like a wiper blade taking lazy swipes at a rain-covered windshield. Lucy, another cat, pokes her nose in. Before our conversation ends, Ruby, an all-black princess, slips into view.

Elana, initially by preference, later out of necessity, goes by Lana. It's only after all our interview sessions are completed that she lets me know she uses a shortened version of her name—Lana. She didn't correct me until I glanced at an email that she'd signed and asked, "Is it Elana or Lana?"

"Lana," she tells me, "I go by Lana."

For most of her life, people mispronounced the name, calling her "E-lay-nah" instead of "E-lah-nah," the Hebrew pronunciation of that name. Deployed to Afghanistan and Iraq as a counterintelligence soldier, her job was to gather information by interrogating locals. Using her Hebrew name wasn't a good way to win hearts and minds. Strict Wahhabis believe that all those who don't practice their form of Islam are heathens and enemies. Lana, more than just an American woman soldier, is a Jewish woman. She needed locals to trust her. Without their cooperation, her complex mission—discovering the whereabouts of bombmaking factories and finding the actual bombmakers before they deployed their lethal handiwork—was next to impossible. Hiding her heritage while deployed, using the shortened secular name Lana, gave her more advantage.

Her motivations to join the military, multifaceted, came together like Sebastian Junger's *The Perfect Storm*. Sequestered and bored in a cramped work cubicle, poring over engineering blueprints and designs, young, intelligent, curious, already with a love of travel and adventure; the clouds of discontent grew. Appreciative of her education and a well-paying engineering job, even as most of the country struggled through the 2002 recession. But being shuttered in a windowless cubicle caged her lust for adventure. Restless and spurred on by those closest to her, a country caught up in a patriotic payback, and a zest for life well beyond the castle keep of a professional engineering career, the military seemed to offer more of what she hungered for. And so, much to the surprise of her parents, she enlisted.

"Telling my parents that I'd enlisted, that's a day I remember well," she said.

"Lana," her father had said, "when I finished college, the Vietnam War had been raging for a few years. I almost certainly would have been drafted. Enlisting gave me options, the ability to choose the military job I wanted, rather than simply getting swallowed up in the infantry. Getting drafted isn't something hanging over your head. You sure about this?"

"I am," she said.

"Then I guess those engineering degrees are going to be the two most expensive pieces of paper I ever paid for."

"I know. I'm sorry, but engineering is boring."

"I know your mom and I won't be able to talk you out of it, so go."

They talked more. The conversation turned lighthearted. They teased each other about degrees and schools—Lana having earned her engineering degrees at Cornell, her father, an English degree at Brown. Lana, like everyone at Cornell, poked fun at Brown. She teased him about his English degree, something Cornell engineering grads considered a bachelor's in bullshit. But back then, that English degree kept her father out of the infantry. He worked at Armed Forces Radio, and later went into news media.

With blessings from her parents (they later loved being able to brag at synagogue about their soldier daughter), Lana enlisted in September, 2002, a year after the September 11 attacks by the terrorist group Al-Qaeda. She signed on for her first hitch, choosing Counterintelligence, later renamed Human Intelligence Collection and Interrogation.

Another piece of the puzzle: Lana's boyfriend Ivan (later husband, later ex-husband) and his two brothers were all enlisting. Ivan's two brothers joined the Marine Corps. Ivan enlisted in the Army. Lana thought that reserves might be a good start, but Ivan had other ideas. When he decided to go active duty, she kicked the idea around, too.

"Maybe active duty's not such a bad plan," she had said. "And hell, Ivan, you don't think I'm going to let you have all the fun."

The desire to become a pilot, perhaps even an astronaut, pushed Lana into engineering. Bad eyes altered her plans. But even with two engineering degrees, she passed on Officer Candidate School. When I asked why, she jokingly claimed to dislike the trappings that came with a commission. "Yeah, I always tell people I didn't like money or respect," she joked. But she also reasoned that if she did like Army life, decided to make the Army a career, she could always become an officer. Understanding first-hand what enlisted life was all about, *that* experience, she knew wouldn't be something she'd learn during OCS.

Impatient, Lana had to wait out a six-month delayed entry into the Army. She reported to Fort Jackson in Columbia, South Carolina on April 15, 2003. The morning of her first wake-up in the Army, Lana turned twenty-three. She was in good company. Fort Jackson, one the Army's many Initial Entry Training facilities—"boot camp" to most of us—was the post of some famous people, including Sgt. Leonard Nimoy (*Star Trek*'s Spock), and Pvt. Jim Croce, the popular folk singer of the '70s.

At the time, women were still denied official roles in combat, even though the Army had already fully integrated. In boot camp, women and men trained side by side. The only separation, the only time apart, came at night after lights-out —they were housed on different floors of the same buildings. During the day the lines blurred. Women and men ran the obstacle course, crawled through mud, learned hand-to-hand combat techniques, and fired weapons—together. Two of Lana's drill sergeants were women.

Boot camp, the laborious, centuries-old *de rigueur* of learning all things military, moved along without any significant events or incidents. Shouts of "drop and gimme fifty," "mark time, mark," "double-time, march!" assaulted the ears of everyone, Lana included.

For Lana and most women, everyday uniforms were an issue. There were no combat fatigues for women. Lana's combat fatigues, a men's small, dwarfed her five-foot-four body. (Now, depending on what leg she is wearing, she can raise up to dizzying heights of five-five, even five-six). The baggy pants and sleeves of the combat fatigues hindered her movements, especially the movement of her arms. It was like trying to move inside a giant paper bag.

On the grenade range, she made the instructor queasy. When it came time to throw a grenade, she asked the range instructor, "Are sure about this? Because I don't think, at least with these loose sleeves, that I'm going to get this thing very far." The instructor, eyes wide, his face suddenly pale, suggested that Lana toss the grenade underhand into a nearby bunker target, just like a bocce ball. The grenade arced gracefully, bounced, then rolled into the bunker. Lana and the instructor ducked behind sandbags. "As I remember it now," she said, "he got down pretty quick."

Lana successfully completed boot camp and AIT, married Ivan, and just a few months later deployed to Afghanistan.

New Foot Day

People with two feet buy new shoes. For Lana, when a prosthetic foot wears out or the stainless-steel peg imbedded into the bone in her leg—the peg her foot snaps onto—needs work, it's "New Foot Day." Peggy (that's the name Lana gave to the peg) meant the end of wearing skinny jeans. New Foot Day began with a trip to the Manhattan Veterans Amputee Clinic, a facility well-known for their wizardry with prosthetics.

On her way to the clinic, Lana shouldered a rumpled canvas tote bag full of shoes, prosthetic feet, and the specialty tools she'd become adept at using. Inside the clinic, she plopped the tote bag onto a work table, then shook the contents loose. A jumble of what looked like mannequin feet, the toes painted red, a hiking and running shoe, a checkered walking shoe, other fake foot paraphernalia, spilled onto the table, clanking and clicking as the detritus fell into a pile.

Replicas of Lana's missing foot were stuffed into a few of the shoes. Stainless-steel posts resembling chess pawns jutted from the centers of the feet.

Memories of the day she injured the now-missing foot spilled out of her just as easily as the prosthetics scattered over the tabletop. Not long after returning from Afghanistan, Lana deployed to Iraq, attached to the 100th Battalion/442nd Infantry Regiment, a unit staffed with reservists from Hawaii, American Samoa, Guam, Saipan, and Washington. The 100th/442nd is unofficially nicknamed the Purple Heart Battalion, with the motto "Remember Pearl Harbor."

Lana loved the big Samoan guys. They were giants, real sweet, special men, but way too protective. She would tell them over and over not to worry about her, or treat her any differently than one of the guys. They couldn't. When she asked why, one of them told her Samoan boys, from a young age, are raised to protect women. "It's ingrained in my heritage," he told her. He just didn't know anything different.

Some of the Samoans called Lana "little girly."

"I'll carry you in my pocket, little girly," one of them once said.

Once, on patrol in 110 degrees, one of those big Samoans was about to pass out from the heat. Lana took the heavy radio he was carrying. shouldered it with her own gear, and carried it for him. "I can carry the radio," she said. "But if you pass out, I can't catch you, you'll squash me like a bug."

In mid-September 2005, not far from Bayji, the highway bustled with late-day traffic. Lana, in full battle rattle, found sitting securely in the backseat of the Humvee difficult. The bulky gear forced her to lean forward, creating space between her and the back of the seat. Her seatbelt lay untethered near her side. The day's mission, interrogating locals in a nearby town, had been another frustrating rendition of the 1950s Abbott and Costello comedy sketch "Who's on First?"

While she talks, her eyes close. She pushes her head into

the back of the couch, pauses, lets out a short sigh then rubs her temples, massaging the past. Collected, she continues, coaxing the day from her memory. "We were near Bayji," she remembers. "Intel spotters had tipped us off that a bad guy, a local insurgent named Hamid or Hamza, memory is fuzzy on the name, would be in a nearby town. Missions were always the same mind-numbing exercise in the absurd. Most days we rolled out of the wire at zero dark thirty, returned near midnight, and rolled out again the next morning. Twenty-hour missions were not unusual.

"It's funny," she said. "Sometimes the location would be a bigger town, more often a mud hut village, but when we'd get there, mud hut or house, village or town, the scene was always the same. We'd show up in a small convoy, four vehicles. We'd dismount, infantry would secure the vehicles, clear houses, and provide security for me, my interpreter, and anyone else with me. The locals always knew what we were there for. For the most part these extremists were not their friends. We wanted to find the bad guys before bombs would go off, killing locals and military, not discriminating. We were clear. We'd roll up in military vehicles, MRAPs, trucks, Humvees. We're always in full battle rattle, armed, turret gunners, tactical. But we never went to the same house, tried never to question the same families, did our best to protect those who would give us information. Still, most missions ended the same, with little or nothing to show for it."

The house or mud hut was always a place filled with generations of family, wives, kids, grandparents, uncles—but never the bad guy the interrogation team was looking for. The conversation, the who's-on-first comedy routine, would sound like this:

"Where is Hamid?"

"Who?"

"Hamid."

"Yes. Yes. Hamid, yes."

"Is he here?"

"Who is here?"

"Hamid."

"Ah, Hamid, yes."

"Wait, do you mean he's here?"

"Who is here?"

"Hamid."

"No. No, Hamid. Hamid go to Baghdad. You just miss him."

"Why'd he go to Baghdad?"

"Who?"

"Hamid."

"Hamid go to Baghdad; I already tell you. For work, he go for work. You come back next week, maybe he is here."

"How is it I always just miss him?"

"Who?"

"Hamid."

"Hamid's in Baghdad, I just tell you."

Frustrated with the *Saturday Night Live* skit, Lana and the team passed out candy to kids, thanked the locals, and now, late in the day, they mounted up. Rolling out on the infamous Highway 1, they began the return to base, hot chow, showers, and safety.

Highway 1 runs between the Jordan border and the Iraqi capital. The highway is asphalted. U.S. convoys faced miles of lawless road prowled by Islamic militias. The return to base, a late-day trek in the thick of Iraqi rush-hour traffic, passed through stretches dubbed "the highway through hell," controlled by the Islamist extremists. It's an adrenaline-pumping journey. Nobody relaxes.

The four-vehicle convoy was rolling at a good speed. Convoy trucks, it didn't matter what type—Humvee, RSOV (Ranger Special Operations Vehicle based on the Land Rover Defender), MRAP, or an up-armored vehicle, they're heavy. Convoys are targets. For that reason, they move out at high speeds, stopping for nothing. Slowing down makes them easy targets. Iraqi drivers know enough to pull over and let the convoy pass.

Lana was in the first vehicle, a Humvee.

As the Humvee rolled up on a Toyota Hilux pickup, a "jingle truck," decorated with pom-poms, and bells, and beads along the bottom of the truck and surrounding the inside windshield, the Humvee driver laid on the horn, the signal for the Iraqis to move over. Eight, maybe ten, Iraqis were in the truck bed, some sitting on the rail of the truck. For all anyone in the convoy knew, the Iraqis could have an RPG laying on the floor of the truck bed. The truck, not moving over, began to slow down. Pickup trucks and stolen Humvees are the ambush vehicle of choice by Islamic bad guys.

Everyone in the Humvee white-knuckled their weapons. Any click of the slide on the 50-caliber would have been drowned out, lost in the whine of the tires and rushing wind. An aging, rusted maroon Toyota Camry in front of the jingle truck began to weave in and out of its lane. It slowed and fell back, suddenly even with the Humvee, then sped up, looking as if the driver was trying to slip in between the convoy and the pickup, classic ambush maneuvering.

Blocked behind the jingle truck, the Camry pulled out, sped up and ducked in front of the truck, almost stopping. The Hilux slammed into the Camry. Up-armored and heavy, rolling at more than eighty kilometers per hour, the Humvee had nowhere to go. Unable to stop, tires screeching their complaint, it plowed into the Iraqi pickup, driving the Camry into a small, slow-moving front-loader that until now had been obscured from sight.

Glass littered the road. Gas and oil spilled from the Iraqi vehicles and puddled on the asphalt. Iraqis were thrown from the pickup. The booming echo of the metal smashing and tearing hung on the air. Steam from ruptured hoses filled

Lana's nose with the sweet, sickening smell of antifreeze. Smoke trailed into the air. Blood colored the highway.

The force of the crash sheared off the right front of the Humvee, rendering the vehicle inoperable. The impact drove Lana's foot under an unyielding metal seat in front of her. She smashed her ankle into a useless M-16 rifle bracket. There are no airbags in an Army Humvee. There is, however, plenty of naked metal and glass. Ligaments in Lana's foot tore. Tendons, muscles, and soft tissue ruptured. The tip of the ankle, that cone-shaped bone covered with the thinnest layer of skin, splintered into small fragments. Thrown against the rear of the Humvee, Lana slammed the back of her head into the metal behind her. Concussed and momentarily stunned, she relied on adrenaline, training, and instinct. She exited the Humvee and took up a tactical position near the right front, the two o'clock position. Pain radiated from her foot into her leg. *Something's not right,* she said to herself. But in the urgency of the moment, she ignored the pain. The driver secured the ten. The turret gunner scanned the area. The Humvee behind them secured the six.

With miles of desert to the right and towns or villages to the left, the convoy was particularly vulnerable. Still uncertain if the accident was a possible attack gone horribly wrong, or nothing more than the outcome of an impatient Iraqi hurrying home to supper, the soldiers maintained an aggressive defensive alert, each taking responsibility for defending strategic sectors of fire.

Lana fought back against the pain.

Blood pooled beneath the bodies of Iraqis scattered on the highway. The driver of the front loader, thrown from the machine, died on the ground. Anxious to get home, the Camry driver, not militants, had caused the accident. The members of the convoy switched from defensive posture, rendering first aid, trying to save lives.

With no chance of returning to the larger base at Bayji,

the Humvee was towed to a nearby FOB. The medical team there examined everyone. Without X-ray equipment, they diagnosed and treated Lana for a sprained ankle. Given plenty of Motrin, 800mg tablets affectionately dubbed "Army candy," she was sent on her way.

"Take two now," the doctor said. "Later, take what you need to manage the pain."

So, numbed with enough pain meds to make her giddy, Lana tightened up her boot and returned to full duty. No one asked about a possible head injury.

Over the next several days the pain and swelling in her foot, getting worse, signaled something more serious than an ankle sprain—signals Lana blocked out. The headache less-ened. Unwilling to appear weak, an unwarranted stereotypical judgement of women serving, Lana didn't complain about pain radiating from her foot. The dizziness she'd felt from slamming her head had gone away. She had a steady supply of Motrin, and no trouble getting more, so she managed the pain in her foot. If it swelled too much, she loosened up the laces of her boot. She even thought about getting a bigger boot. She kept quiet and resumed missions.

"The worst thing for me," she said, "having been in-coun-try, going out with my guys every day, would have been to get pulled offline, not to be able to go out on missions. This was what I signed up for, and I wanted to do my job. I was good at it. And—I didn't want to let my guys down. I didn't want them to go out without me. And I knew if I didn't, I'd be victim of the pervasive thinking, that women can't endure pain the way men can."

So, managing the pain, disguising the injury to her foot with the 800mg Motrins, Lana just kept going. The few times she visited the infirmary, medics or doctors reasoned that she was walking well enough despite the pain. They told her, "It'll get better with time," dispensed more Motrin, jokingly told her to rub a little dirt on it, and sent her on her way. Over time, bone fragments fused, untreated ligament and tendon damage became permanent, pain grew increasingly chronic. Continually told that her foot would get better, Lana stopped seeking treatment, coped with the pain and, in order to continue to serve, hid her symptoms—until years later, when treatment and a cure would be too late. Then, the only option was amputation. But that came later. Back out on missions, happy to be with her guys, Lana continued to interrogate Iraqi villagers.

The usual routine was punctuated with an event too bizarre to explain away, even if one subscribed to the catch-all "It ain't nothing, it's just Iraq" explanation for the unexplainable, the nonsensical, the unbelievable. During one interrogation, the village elder disappeared, later returning with two camels, a small herd of goats (maybe ten, Lana guessed), and two of his three wives. Animated, talking excitedly, pointing at Lana, then to the camels and goats, he seemed intent on making some sort of deal. He pulled one wife forward. The squad leader shook his head, a clear *no*. The elder pulled the second wife forward. Lana asked the interpreter what the elder was up to.

"He wants to trade the camels, goats, and one of the wives for you. He wants to marry you," the interpreter said. "The sergeant is negotiating."

"What?"

"Yeah, he's negotiating."

Lana turned to the squad leader. "Hey," she said. "Tell him he has enough trouble with the wives he has. Tell him I'll nag him to death. And two camels, and some scrawny goats, that's not even close. And one more thing."

"Yeah?"

"Really dude, you're playing along with this guy? Really?"

IED! IED! IED!

In early fall, two weeks after she injured her foot, and fore-warned about the possibility of several IEDs planted near the base, Lana's four-vehicle convoy rolled out of the wire not long after sunrise. Lana, the driver, vehicle commander, and interpreter were sardined inside an M1114 Humvee. The turret gunner manned his perch. In the 100-plus degrees, rolling out with the air rushing by, the heat hit him like a hairdryer blowing in his face.

Lana rode in the second Humvee, back seat, passenger side. The convoy ignored the sound of several explosions, a cache of seized IEDs deliberately being detonated in a blast pit on the base. Route-clearing units kept roads entering and exiting the base as clear and as safe as possible. Berms of shoveled earth, ten-to-twenty-foot-high sloped barriers, bordered both sides of the roads, the perfect place for planting and burying IEDs. Militants secreted themselves behind and near the top of the berms, watching and waiting for a convoy to enter the kill zone, detonating the IED when they felt certain they could inflict damage, even mass casualties. Spotters had warned of three planted IEDs along the road exiting the base. Clearing units found two. Twenty mikes outside the wire, Lana's convoy found the third.

Hearing the blast, the soldiers tucked inside the Humvees thought they'd heard another controlled blast from the base. But a trigger man had waited for the first Humvee to pass, then detonated a large, wired explosive, maybe a rocket or large artillery round with a blast plate that directed the explosion toward its intended target. Time suspended for a split second before the blast wave lifted the Humvee and blew Lana back and forth like a ragdoll. She saw dust bloom into a blast cloud. She saw the fireball. She heard the thunder of the explosion. She heard Sergeant Tupelo, the vehicle commander, yelling into the radio, "IED! IED! IED!" Shrapnel peppered the right side of the Humvee. Clumps of dirt rained down, their syncopated thuds sounding like the bass beats of a dozen timpani.

Lana's Humvee stopped. The lead vehicle rolled forward to escape a potential kill zone. Vehicles behind her backed up quickly, getting to the X spot, a predesignated tactical position. Slammed into the metal backstop behind her, then whiplashed forward, Lana's world went dark. The driver turned and shook Lana, jarring her conscious. She looked down at the hand rocking her leg back and forth. *He shouldn't be turned around, he knows better,* she said to herself. *Why is he doing that? I'm okay. Who is he anyway?*

Still dazed, Lana struggled to make sense of everything. *What's happening to me? Who are these strange men? Where am I?* Everything around her played out like a well-choreographed movie shoot. Men scrambled from the Humvee, reacting, going tactical. Lana's eyes darted from one soldier to the next. She struggled to pull herself out of the seat, rose up a few inches, then collapsed.

Trained, like all soldiers, to take a few seconds and evaluate her condition, Lana reasoned that she had all her limbs. She ordered herself to evacuate the Humvee. Her body disobeyed the command. She looked around, watching the others. Nothing made sense. She wondered who all the men were, why were they shouting, running? She raised a hand to her face, felt something warm, wet, sticky. Rivulets of blood trailed down her cheeks. She was bleeding from her ears, most likely her nose too. She wasn't sure. Slowly, very slowly she began to remember who she was, where she was, and to worry.

Maybe I am injured. Am I? Disoriented for sure. Just fake it girl, c'mon, fake it till you make it. Get out of the vehicle. Snap out of it. Can't remember names, then just call everyone by their rank. That's it, slip out of the seat, slide out of the Humvee. Oh crap, don't fall. Grab onto something. Steady yourself. Follow the others just follow. Stay upright.

Outside of the vehicle, Lana willed herself to function. The squad raced up the berm ready to engage, waiting for small-arms fire that never came. Lana stumbled after them. Without the threat of further attack, the soldiers reached the crest of the berm, and scrambled over the top in pursuit of the disappearing bomber. Lana, still hobbled by the two-week old foot injury, shaken from the blast, dazed and dizzy, fell down the slope of the berm, trying hopelessly to catch herself.

An hour later, medics and squad leaders, believing that no one had been seriously injured (the turret gunner, shrapnel to his hand, got the most attention), decided to resume the day's mission. Lana's team rolled up to a house where the local Iraqi, the source of the day's interrogation, lived. Still dazed, believing that the team was setting up a checkpoint, Lana took up a tactical position once the vehicle stopped, forgetting that she'd spent the past three months developing the local Iraqi as a possible informant. Her erratic behavior got the attention of her battle buddy, a large Samoan soldier. He took over the interrogation. Lana settled outside of the house, drifting off while the other soldier completed the interrogation.

By nightfall the convoy returned to base. Lana, still dizzy, head now throbbing, vision blurry, and more disoriented than earlier in the day, went untreated. She should have died. The injury caused a hemorrhage to her brain. Her brain swelled under the pressure of the bleeding. Some of the blood, enough of it to reduce the swelling in her brain, seeped into a small hollow space, a then-undiscovered anomaly that saved her life. The bleeding slowed. Blood began to thicken and clot. The bleeding stopped. The confusion, disorientation, memory loss, headaches did not.

Three days after the attack, still not herself, not receiving intensive care and life-saving surgery, unable to convince medical that she wasn't wigged out, or emotionally over-whelmed by the attack, Lana was flagged to report to mental health. Psych had the ability to pull her off-line, but Lana, a trained interrogator, played the game, telling them what she thought they wanted to hear. Her determination and the misdiagnosis became her worst enemies.

She knew now that she'd been injured by the blast, but increasingly refused to show it or agree with medical that she'd been psychologically overwhelmed by the attack. Lana, like most of the women she served with, were constantly judged. Held to a higher standard, Lana knew that she had to prove her worth, not just this once, but over and over and over. So in between visits to mental health, she continued to go out on missions. "I'm worth it," she told herself. "I'm worth being part of this team."

At night, she had trouble sleeping. During the day, she found it difficult to keep track of anything. Her memory, once borderline photographic, diminished. She compensated by writing everything down. Determined to hide the changes to her memory, she kept notes on scraps of paper, pads, her sleeve, jotted things down on her hand, her arms—anywhere. At some point, she tattooed lines on her left arm, turning the forearm into a notepad.

Her tour ended just a month after the attack. It would be her last deployment to a war zone. Two and a half years would pass before the brain injury that should have killed her on the day of the IED attack was finally diagnosed. She kept taking 800mg Motrin tablets for her foot.

Now What?

After coming home from Iraq, Lana visited family, briefly reunited with her husband Ivan, and deployed to Germany. Out of the ten years they'd be married, Lana and Ivan managed little more than three of those years together. Eventually the time apart doomed any chance that the marriage would work.

For more than two years, she hid the lingering effects of the head and foot injuries. Between Motrin and a high tolerance to pain, she coped with the foot injury. She masked the changes in her physical and mental abilities, put a lid on her emotions and, when asked by those closest to her what was wrong, she repeatedly replied, "Nothing." She compensated, wrote everything down, managed the frequent migraines with meds, wore sunglasses more often to hide a lazy eye and a new sensitivity to light. To most people, even those who knew her well, she got by. The swindle, like almost every ruse, eventually ran its course.

A neurologist at Landstuhl Regional Medical Center (LRMC), the Army's largest American military hospital outside the continental United States, became familiar with Lana's medical history. The trail was littered with visits to medical for headaches, blurry vision, occasional dizziness. He was one of the few doctors looking into blast wave concussion injuries, and he suspected that Lana had sustained a brain injury during the 2005 attack. Ordering an MRI, he quickly confirmed his suspicions. The hemorrhaged blood that had clotted had left behind an area of dead brain tissue.

He operated, removing part of Lana's brain.

Having already made up her mind that she'd make a career out of the Army, maybe use her degrees to get a pair of butter bars, Lana's major concern now was to avoid a medical evaluation board (MEB). She'd been flying under the radar, hiding changes that surgery and a medical record could now reveal. So, after recovering from the initial surgery, Lana plunged herself into a more rigorous physical and mental rehab back in the U.S. at Walter Reed. Working hard at rehab, she regained some of her original mobility, coordination, vision, memory, and speech.

When Lana deployed to Hawaii, joining an elite intelligence unit, Ivan left the Army and returned to civilian life. Lana appeared to be a fit soldier. While Iraq was winding down, Afghanistan heated up. With a divorce almost certain, nothing anchoring her to anyone or any one place, and still hungry for adventure, she volunteered to redeploy to Afghanistan. That's where the problem began. Doctors assessing her mental and physical fitness for deployment would poke and prod. Mentally, questions required simple precise answers, no spinning off, no getting cute or creative. Physically, vision, strength, balance, coordination, all would have to meet minimum standards—

The doctor's words came at her in staccato bursts—some side conditions—limited peripheral vision—recurring migraines—possibly unfit for active duty as a result of brain trauma—

"Stop, that's enough," she said. But there was more.

"I'm recommending a medical evaluation board," the doctor said.

The words reverberated with a hollow echo. Panic coursed through her. She knew that all it would take was for just one doctor to find something in her list of conditions that triggered a regulation. In the cover-your-ass military world, no one is checking the box "fit for duty" if there are issues, even one. A med-board rarely erred in favor of the soldier. For Lana, there were a host of potential issues. Any one of them, on individual merit, would easily disqualify her as fit for the duties of a soldier. Lana left the medical center, knowing she'd be forced to medically retire. She sat on a beach, waiting for nightfall and the impending doom of the uncompromising medical evaluation board.

She'd run out of places to hide.

By the spring of 2011, the Army ordered Lana to Maryland. The medical evaluation board commenced at Walter Reed Military Medical Center. Lana, always one to push back, submitted herself to the physical trespass of the medical assessment team. The final decision dragged on. After the completed physical at the start of the board, all the paperwork was sent to the regional medical board. Days turned into weeks, months. Helpless, Lana fumed. Her records sat in a black hole for a year, buried in the tomb of military bureaucracy.

She filed a rebuttal, fought the review board for a year, but even before the verdict was rendered, the Army had made it clear that Lana would never deploy to a combat zone—never. Even if she could, winning the rebuttal would chain her to a desk—again.

When someone finally resurrected her records, the medical assessment team performed a quick, perfunctory review of the paperwork. The final decision, based on the medical board's assessment of Lana's medical condition and the impact of her injuries, deemed her unfit for the job of a soldier. She had joined the Army almost on a whim, fell in love with soldiering, and had decided to make the military her life-long professional career. So, now what?

Finding a Path

Medically retired from active duty in December 2012, civilian life thrust upon her, her career abruptly ended, Lana had no clear path in front of her. She'd given the past ten years of her life to the Army, and spent the last year not knowing if and when she'd be sent packing. Now that the final verdict was in, she had less than ninety days to get ready for the rest of her life. She thought about a career with the FBI. She did, after all, have a bachelor's and master's in engineering and ten years of enlisted service in intelligence and interrogation. She'd been in highly specialized and secretive units, but being medically retired due to combat injuries meant she couldn't qualify for field agent work, not even a desk job in the iconic federal agency.

For almost seven years, the Army had denied her a Purple Heart. Fed up, she decided to fight. She won that battle. She reasoned that she could not be retired for combat injuries without qualifying for a Purple Heart. Simple college freshman logic. So before she officially retired, she received the recognition due her.

Reality hit her like the blast from the IED. Just a few weeks before the new year, late in December of 2012, former Army Sergeant Elana Duffy had no job, no insurance, was recently divorced, and temporarily homeless. She'd left behind the close network of friends she'd made in the military. Unwilling to rely on family, she came back to NYC, a few miles from where she grew up, hoping familiar terrain would be easier to maneuver. Not certain of her benefits, less certain of where to look, who to contact, unable to connect with others who'd been through the same thing, she stumbled.

The security of being part of a military unit where soldiers looked out for one another disappeared like the flash of the IED that had changed her life. Suddenly on her own, Lana struggled. She drifted, bouncing between different programs, looking for a place to fit, not certain of what she needed, even more unwilling to admit that she might need help.

She began to volunteer with some of the organizations she'd approached. She dabbled at a few engineering gigs just to put food on the table. The more veterans she came into contact with, the more she realized that her situation was a common predicament experienced by many returning veterans.

"The situation," as she described it, "was endemic."

Friends began attempting suicide. Some succeeded. Lana had an engineering background and disability income to rely on, resources that gave her the means and time to figure out her life. Others weren't so fortunate. She knew that there were many programs and resources for returning veterans, but many were cookie-cutter, a one-size-fits-all that veterans, already reluctant to ask for and accept help, resented. Any simple thing could turn a veteran away. A brusque remark, a long wait, a bad experience, a program that didn't address the need, and most veterans walked out of a facility, never to return or look elsewhere.

"This," Lana said, "is particularly true among veterans with mental health issues. One bad experience is all it takes for someone to say 'I guess this isn't for me' and they usually quit looking."

Lana took action. Transitioning back to civilian life shouldn't be so hard. There had to be an easier path. She'd walked point on the trail of the returning veteran. Sharing what she learned would allow others to follow safely. Using the experience of her personal struggle with returning to civilian life, she was determined to make life easier for those coming after her.

She started working with individuals at an NYU veteran entrepreneur program to frame out some ideas. She collaborated with a Navy veteran, a guy named Mike. Got him on board. Mike used his background, modern data engineering, to work on the "fit" problem, matching the right program with the right veteran, and to track trends.

Lana also contemplated how to figure out how to help someone identify what they needed before it became a real problem. Her engineering degrees are in Operations Research Engineering, which is now largely data science. The data, the information for veterans, was out there, but it was often difficult to find. She put her engineering background to work—only this time she wasn't sequestered in a cubicle, pouring over prints and plans. This time, ignited by a passion to help others, she cobbled together a team of professionals and engineered a solution, an easily accessible database of resources for veterans, families and caregivers. She founded and built her own company, Pathfinder Labs, a company focused on helping veterans and their families through what sometimes is a difficult transition from active duty back into civilian life.

Wounded in action, denied the career she loved by a roadside bomb, and having a foot amputated didn't stop this former Army sergeant. None of those things could. Lana Duffy is so much more than the bad things that happened.

A LETTER TO READERS

MARY SILLER SCULLIN

A FEW MONTHS after our youngest brother, NYC firefighter Stephen Siller, sacrificed his life on 9/11, my siblings and I formed the Tunnel to Towers Foundation. The mission was to honor Stephen and all those who perished on that fateful day. The cornerstone of what we would become was based on the words of St. Francis, "Brothers and sisters, while we have time, let us do good." As a Foundation, we have been guided by his words. We have found the greatest love and the greatest joy working to bring hope into the lives of our military and first-responder families facing catastrophic injuries or death in the line of duty.

We have met the most beautiful, dedicated, selfless people on our journey. We have been privileged to support the greatest American heroes who have come home from war without limbs, burned, battling traumatic brain injuries and more. We have also been blessed to have come to know the unsung heroes—spouses—who have sacrificed so much with the loss of their loved ones who died in the line of duty.

There is one recurring, ever-present thread that runs through each and every encounter: Love. Love of God. Love of family. Love of country.

While Ron Farina was writing his book *Who Will Have My Back*, I was fortunate to sit with Ron and share my thoughts and feelings about the loss of my brother and about the special people my family has met through the work of the Foundation. It was a very reflective experience. I felt Ron's presence was thoughtful and tender throughout my interview with him. I knew my story was in good hands.

In the book you are reading, *Out of the Shadows: Voices of American Women Soldiers*, Ron's simple and respectful approach in recounting the incredible lives of the women you just met is a precious gift Ron is able to give to readers.

St. Francis, most known for his Prayer of Peace, was very notably ahead of the times (not just 13th-century times, but sadly, even today!). I love that his Canticle praises not only Brother Sun but Sister Moon as well. *Out of the Shadows* is modern day praise for Sister Moon. St. Francis entrusted his deepest spiritual longings to his counterpart in religious life, St. Clare. They worked together, they prayed together. It was rare. The relationship, the responsibility and respect St. Francis had for St. Clare pulled her out of the shadows into the light.

Out of the Shadows, this beautiful compilation of stories of American women soldiers, highlights their bravery, their dedication and their willingness to sacrifice life and limb for us. It is a blessing to have the light shine on their extraordinary lives and acknowledge their vital role in protecting their fellow Americans.

We are still in an infancy stage when it comes to awareness of the profound impact women have made in many areas of life, but none as striking as their role in war. I am saddened that this book is "one of a kind" and unique in the history of war stories.

It is such a privilege to be given this chance to meet these great American women warriors, who have put themselves on the line for us. I am humbled and I am grateful to Ron for helping these wonderful women bring their military journeys into the light of day. May their stories ignite a plethora of other tales of remarkable women in war, who can inspire us and serve as role models for us all.

Mary Siller Scullin
Chief Administrative Officer
Stephen Siller Tunnel to Towers Foundation
Staten Island, New York
December 29, 2021

AFTERWORD

The idea for *Out of the Shadows: Voices of American Women Soldiers* came to me after the publication of *Who Will Have My Back*, a book that focused on individuals and organizations dedicated to the care of America's veterans catastrophically wounded in Iraq and Afghanistan.

Some readers commented that book did not mention or feature stories about wounded women soldiers. The omission was unintentional, an unwitting slight. I hadn't thought about whether women soldiers (I use the term soldiers to include all branches of the military) were written about with the same frequency as their male counterparts. So, to see for myself, I visited larger, well-known bookstores, scouring rows of books for stories about American women serving in Iraq and Afghanistan. The shelves in the sections on war were stacked with books about battles, and the soldiers who fought in them. The heroes were almost always men.

To be fair, there were a few, but not enough. On occasion, a book like Tammy Duckworth's memoir, *Every Day is a Gift*, would be prominently at the entrance to my local Barnes and Nobles, but where were the stories of the thousands of everyday women who fought, in Afghanistan and Iraq? Even the plethora of stories on the Internet seemed like well-kept secrets, and were often nothing more than a reposting of internet newspaper articles.

I later discovered, while interviewing the women for this book, that many of the internet articles and stories were crafted without interviewing the veteran herself, and contained many inaccuracies.

I wanted to do more. The idea for *Out of the Shadows* blossomed into what would become a year-and-a-half undertaking, a book about wounded American women soldiers. With the personal and financial support of Duke Leopold d'Arenberg the project took shape. Oren Litwin, editor/publisher of Lagrange Books who had helped produce *Who Will Have My Back*, signed on as well. I contacted researcher Donald Collins. Donald was relentless in his pursuit of veterans for this book. He soon put me in touch with dozens of wounded American women soldiers. I talked to each one. Many declined to participate. I interviewed about twenty women soldiers; thirteen agreed to move forward. Along the way, four of the women, their memories too painful or too elusive, declined to go further. Nine remained. Nine told their stories. They came from every part of the country: California, Connecticut, Illinois, Arizona, South Dakota, Washington, D.C. Alaska, Texas, and New York City.

Each had her own reason, her why of becoming a soldier and deploying to Afghanistan or Iraq, or in some instances, to both theaters on a second or third deployment. Being a soldier became a link in the chain of their DNA.

To many readers, the stories of these nine women may have seem too similar. That's because they are. That is the dangerous absurdity of war, a daily, a repetitive pursuit of life and death. These women provided security on and off FOBs, collected intelligence, and rolled out on missions or patrols in up-armored Humvees, usually as a driver or turret gunner. In the heat of an attack, a firefight, an ambush, they were as courageous, brave, skilled, and lethal as any of their male counterparts. And they fought side by side with men while officially banned from combat until 2015.

To gather the information for each story, the women and I spent hours on Zoom. We laughed together. Sometimes we cried. They recounted—often with amazing detail—the good, the bad, and the ugly of their deployments. We traded emails often, talked on the phone when that worked best, and we texted. I often became lost, listening to them recount their experiences. When that happened (they'll tell you it happened often, it did), I'd miss an important point or fail to get a date, a name, a place. The writing would grind to a halt. I'd text the question. Each woman almost always responded within minutes. I'm forever grateful. Once they filled in the gaps, the stories would move forward—until I had another question. I never measured, but I swear some of the text chains had to be a foot long. Because these stories are true, I wanted to get them right.

The few places where memory lessened and details slipped away, I filled in the blanks—writing, I hope, without straying too far. I reimagined the dialogue of many of the supporting characters—other soldiers, interpreters, Afghan and Iraqi locals, officers, medics, doctors, husbands, wives, parents. I tried in all instances to keep the dialogue consistent with the event.

Each story could easily be a stand-alone memoir. What I've tried to do here was capture enough of each woman's time in Iraq or Afghanistan, and their time as a soldier. When I asked each of these women if they would tell their story, they said yes, adding that they'd be honored. I hope the stories honor them.

These women are courageous, strong, smart, resilient, beautiful—*Audacious!*

—Ron Farina

ABOUT THE AUTHOR

Ron Farina is author of two previous books, *At the Altar of the Past* and *Who Will Have My Back*. Other works include *Unsung Heroes, Keeping Promises,* and *Worn Torn,* personal essays about the human cost of war. In 2021 he was awarded the AWP Intro Award for fiction. He lives in Connecticut with his wife and two Golden Retrievers, Henry and Preacher.

He holds an MFA from Western Connecticut State University. He served in Vietnam in 1966-1967.

Ron can be reached at dasherdog1@gmail.com

Made in United States
North Haven, CT
03 December 2022

27758686R00162